Contemporary Techniques for the Bassoon: Multiphonics

Contemporary Techniques for the Bassoon: Multiphonics

Jamie Leigh Sampson

ADJ•ective New Music, LLC

Jamie Leigh Sampson (b. 1984 Syracuse, NY) is a composer and bassoonist living in Northwest Ohio. She holds a bachelor's degree in Music Composition from the State University of New York at Fredonia, and master's degrees in Music Composition and Bassoon Performance from Bowling Green State University.

ADJ•ective New Music, Bowling Green, OH 43402

©2014 by ADJ•ective New Music, LLC

All rights reserved. Published 2014

Printed in the United States of America

For more information regarding ADJ•ective New Music publications please contact:

info@adjectivenewmusicllc.com

www.adjectivenewmusicllc.com

ISBN: 978-0-615-99938-8

Cover art used with permission from iStockphoto.com. Photo of Jamie Leigh Sampson used with permission from Mary Pencheff.

The Neue Bassoon font was designed by Spoke Designs, LLC (Toledo, OH).

    Website: www.spokehq.com

    Email: Gene@spokehq.com

For Mr. Gregory Quick,
who taught me the advantage of learning my mistakes.

Contents

List of Tables

Foreword

I am honored that I was asked to write the Foreword for this important addition to the literature concerning two disciplines that are close to my heart. As a bassoonist and composer, I have long been fascinated by the frequent intersections between these two areas. I obtained a double degree in Bassoon Performance and Composition during my undergraduate studies in New Zealand, and continued with composition lessons and courses through both my master's and doctorate. I also completed a doctoral lecture recital and dissertation on music for bassoon written by bassoonists, and a subsequent CD of works for bassoon and piano by bassoonists. All along I have been involved in writing and performing works that incorporate extended techniques, including multiphonics and harmonics. This book fills a very important niche in explaining and cataloging these techniques on the bassoon, and will greatly aid both bassoonists and composers in utilizing these sounds in creation and performance.

I actually met Jamie at a point of intersection between composition and bassoon. I was a guest composer at the prestigious New Music Festival at Bowling Green State University, where Dr. Nathaniel Zeisler performed my piece *Swamp Song* for bassoon and CD (which incidentally includes a fairly extensive multiphonics section). Dr. Zeisler invited me to present a masterclass for his excellent bassoon studio, and Jamie was one of the participating students. I recall that she performed Leslie Bassett's *Metamorphoses*, and I believe I made various comments that eventually, and indirectly, led her to pursue this line of research further. If that is the case, I am very pleased and grateful, as this book is the result. I am also pleased to be one of twenty bassoonists who tested the nearly four hundred unique multiphonic fingerings that were distilled down to those contained within this resource. I can attest that there were many fingerings that I was not aware of, but that can be very effective on the instrument.

Jamie is herself both an excellent bassoonist and composer, and has done a lot of well-organized and painstaking research in order to create this book. She compiled materials from several pre-existing resources, field-testing each with a number of bassoonists. These bassoonists used different equipment and set-ups in order to determine which sounds can be most dependably reproduced by all players. She presents the results in a clear and logical format.

I share Jamie's hope that this book will be a resource that spurs an expansion of the repertoire and sonic possibilities, through new compositions and performances of bassoon works. I know that I will use this book as a reference for my own bassoon playing and composing, and am confident that others will as well.

Michael Burns

Bassoon Professor, School of Music, Theatre and Dance

The University of North Carolina at Greensboro

March 2014

Acknowledgements

This book would not have been possible without the dedicated team of bassoonists, composers, advisors, editors, and friends that have generously given their time, feedback, support, and enthusiasm. I would be remiss in my duties as an author if I did not extend a public thank you to the first person who suggested that I could write a resource of this magnitude: Burton Beerman, Distinguished Professor of the Arts Emeritus at Bowling Green State University. One day, during a composition lesson, he paused and said, "Someone should write a new multiphonic book for bassoon. You could do it." This research is the result.

Eighteen bassoonists, in addition to myself, tested and/or recorded multiphonics during the various phases of this project. These bassoonists were Tim Abbott, Jonathan Aaron Brown, Michael Burns, Benjamin Coelho, Michael Harley, Rebekah Heller, Dana Jessen, Jeffrey Lyman, Heather MacLean, Susan Nelson, Christopher Porter, Hannah Reilly, Saxton Rose, Chelsea Schumann, Maya Stone, Devon Tipp, Katherine Young, and Nathaniel Zeisler. Each of these bassoonists contributed significantly to the information presented in this book, and I could not have completed this project without them. Their commitment to expanding the repertoire for contemporary bassoonists—through commissions, premieres, education, and participation in projects like this one—is to be admired and commended.

I would like to extend a very special thank you to Miss Betsy Wagner, who helped ensure that seventh grade bassoonists everywhere would be able to play all "Group One" multiphonics!

There were quite a few people who offered technical assistance with audio recording, document layout, and project design. These individuals included Bruce Bartlett, Mark Bunce, Christopher Chandler, and Mikel Kuehn. Their technical expertise made the analysis accurate and effective, and the formatting clear and concise. Special thanks to Gene Powell and Scott Deca of Spoke HQ for their design of Neue Bassoon, the fingering font used throughout this book.

I offer gratitude to Ms. Sipkje Pesnichak and the Merit School of Music for generously donating recording space during the second phase of this project.

The analysis of over three thousand audio files was completed with the assistance of the 2013 ADJ•ective New Music, LLC interns: Ashley Bonner, John J. Pearse, Carter Rice, Michiko Saiki, and Andrew Selle. I wish you every success in your promising careers as performers, composers, conductors, and administrators.

My fellow ADJ•ective Directors, this book is the best it can be because of you. Andrew Martin Smith you are my ever-present partner, friend, and helpful critic; thank you for always grounding me in reality when my ideas sometimes lead me in every direction at once. To my dear friend Molly Fidler, thank you for your insights and our discussions; I could not have completed this endeavor without you!

The support of my family, friends, and mentors has been overwhelming throughout the entire research and writing process. My parents, grandparents, and in-laws—as well as the mentors and friends that I consider family, including Donald and Kathleen Bohlen, Annie Neikirk, Rebekah Valerio, DJ Brady, Daniel Knaggs, Marc Beth, and Amy Riske—have not only provided encouragement, they have eagerly anticipated this book's release with unmatched enthusiasm. For that I will be forever grateful!

Introduction

At her CD[1] release party in July 2013, bassoonist Rebekah Heller said, "The difficulty in playing the bassoon is not in making a sound, it is in making the same sound twice." I believe this statement encapsulates the past fifty years of research regarding contemporary techniques for the bassoon. Composers who write using previously published resources cannot be certain that all of the techniques they select will transfer easily from one bassoon to the next. Bassoonists often spend a great deal of time adapting multiphonic and microtonal fingerings in pre-existing works for their bassoon.

Multiphonic fingerings are particularly difficult to replicate due to variations in instrumental construction worldwide. In addition to the differences between French and German style bassoons, an instrument's bore dimensions, key system, bocal construction, and the performer's reed style contribute to a variety of timbre outcomes. Bassoons do not depreciate as quickly as other woodwind instruments,[2] which results in a remarkably varied field. It is unreasonable to expect one multiphonic fingering, tested on one bassoon, to work on all bassoons.

The aim of this book is to present the most reliable multiphonic fingerings for German bassoons with their corresponding pitch content, embouchure adjustments, dynamic spectrum, and notation suggestions. Existing contemporary technique resources tested multiphonic fingerings on one or two bassoons. Twenty bassoonists from around the United States tested the 369 fingerings included in this study. The performers' expertise ranged from middle school novices to professionals who specialize in contemporary techniques. Instruments from five bassoon manufacturers were included: Heckel, Püchner, Fox (several models), Mooseman, and Yamaha.

As a result of this testing, 271 stable multiphonic fingerings were proven to be reliable across most instruments within the study, while ninety-nine fingerings were too unreliable for publication.[3] The multiphonic fingerings found in *Contemporary Techniques for the Bassoon: Multiphonics* are grouped based on ease of production, and include specific embouchure suggestions from participating bassoonists. While composers should always check with a performer before using a multiphonic in their

---

[1] Rebekah Heller, *100 Names*, Tundra Records 001.

[2] The oldest bassoon included in this research was nearly one hundred years old, while the newest instrument was manufactured approximately ten years ago.

[3] The ninety-nine eliminated fingerings worked on less than half of the bassoons tested.

works, it is my hope that this book eliminates some of the concern regarding sonic fidelity when these multiphonics are performed by additional bassoonists.

As performers and composers formalize the study of multiphonics across the woodwind family, the diversity of bassoons in circulation will maintain a certain level of unpredictability. With this book, however, composers should be able to make informed decisions about specific multiphonics, understand their response issues, and more accurately predict the sonic result of each. Bassoonists will be able to compare pitch content in pre-existing works to find the best fingerings, work with composers on new compositions, and fully explore their standard technique through the development of contemporary techniques.[4]

---

[4] Jamie Leigh Sampson, "Polyvalent Fingerings for the Bassoon: An Introduction," *The Double Reed* 37, no. 1 (2014): 134–142.

Symbols and Abbreviations

Pitch Notation

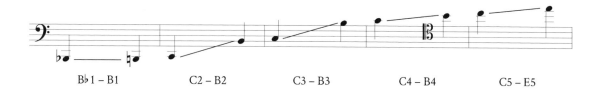

B♭1 – B1   C2 – B2   C3 – B3   C4 – B4   C5 – E5

Microtones

One eighth-tone sharp	♮↑	One eighth-tone flat	♮↓
One quarter-tone sharp	‡	One quarter-tone flat	ⅾ
Three eighth-tones sharp	♯	Three eighth-tones flat	♭
One semitone sharp	♯	One semitone flat	♭
Five eighth-tones sharp	♯	Five eighth-tones flat	♭

Fingerings

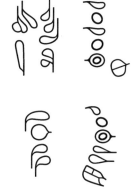

Open key or tonehole	○
Closed key or covered tonehole	●
1/2 hole	◓
Flicked key	♩

Contemporary Techniques for the Bassoon: Multiphonics

1. Methodology

The following methodology outlines the protocol for testing each of the multiphonic fingerings included in this study. To restrict variables, other than those introduced by manufacturing, it was important that each fingering was tested in the same manner by every bassoonist. Table 1 includes details for all of the instruments used in Phase Two and Three of testing.

Table 1. Instruments Used to Test Multiphonic Fingerings

Maker	Model	Year[1]	Phase Two	Phase Three
Fox	III	N/A		(Group One only)
Fox	201	2000	•	
Fox	201	1996	•	
Fox	201	N/A		•
Fox	220	2002	•	
Fox	240	2002	•	•
Fox	240	N/A	•	
Fox	601	1997		'
Fox	601	2008		•
Heckel		1998–2003	•	
Heckel		1933–1936	•	•
Heckel		1924–1927	•	•
Heckel		1919–1924	•	
Heckel		1936–1940		•
Mooseman	220AP/222A	2001	•	•
Püchner	5000	N/A[2]	•	
Püchner		N/A		•
Püchner		1964–1969		•
Püchner		N/A		•
Yamaha	YFG-812	N/A	•	•

[1] Maarten Vonk, *Bundle of Joy* (Amersfoort, Netherlands: FagotAtelier, 2007) 23–42.

[2] All Püchner serial numbers for bassoons made before 1954 were lost. Serial numbers for bassoons made 1955–1964 were not retained. See Maarten Vonk's *Bundle of Joy*.

1.1. Phase One: Collection of Multiphonic Fingerings

A total of 369 multiphonic fingerings were collected and compared from six resources.[3]

- Bartollozzi, Bruno. *New Sounds for Woodwind.* Reginald Smith Brindle, translator. New York: Oxford University Press, 1967.
- Gallois, Pascal. *Techniques of Bassoon Playing.* New York: Barenreiter, 2009.
- International Double Reed Society website, s.v. "Heckel-System (German) Bassoon Multiphonic Fingerings by Note Name" (by Terry Ewell), http://www.idrs.org/resources/BSNFING/fingmult.htm (accessed November 29, 2013).
- Lipp, Charles Herbert. *New Compositional Techniques for the Bassoon.* Doctoral Thesis, University of Illinois at Urbana-Champaign, 1982.
- Penazzi, Sergio. *Metodo Per Fagotto.* Milan: Suvini Zerboni, 1972.
- Leslie Ross's Official Web Site, s.v. "Multiphonics for Modern Bassoon" (by Leslie Ross), http://www.leslieross.net/multiphonics.html (accessed November 29, 2013).

While many fingerings appeared in more than one resource, the International Double Reed Society website is the only one that explicitly states testing two or more bassoons.[4]

1.2. Phase Two: Elimination and Classification of Multiphonic Fingerings

Table 2. Bassoons in Phase Two

Instruments	Number
Heckel	4
Püchner	1
Fox	5
Mooseman	1
Yamaha	1

Table 3. Bassoonists in Phase Two

Bassoonists	Number
Professional	5
Young Professionals & Graduate Students	4
Undergraduate Students	2
High School Students	1

Twelve bassoonists tested the original 369 fingerings. They were asked to indicate whether the fingering did or did not produce a multiphonic on their instrument, document any embouchure manipulations that aided the multiphonic's response, and provide

---

[3] For a complete list of multiphonics and their corresponding resources see Appendix A.

[4] Terry Ewell tested on a Heckel whose serial number places its production date between 1981 and 1986, and Lisa Hoyt tested on a Fox made in 1995.

feedback on the dynamic range.[5] These three factors—successful production of a multiphonic, dynamic range, and prevalence of response issues—were used to classify multiphonics into seven groups.

Table 4. Classification of Multiphonics after Phase Two

Group	Number of Bassoons	Dynamic Range[6]	Response Issues
1	10–12	pp–ff	None
2	10–12	p–f	Some
3	8–9	p–f	Some
4	8–9	mp–mf	Numerous
5	10–12	pp–ff	None
6	6–8	Limited	Numerous
7	5 or fewer	Limited	N/A

The pitch content for Group 5 fingerings changed over the dynamic range. As a bassoonist crescendoed or decrescendoed there was more than one distinct set of pitch content for each fingering. At this stage, they required their own category.

The fingerings in Group 6 required embouchure manipulations that were too drastic. While some changes are necessary, embouchure manipulation should never be so significant that they inhibit the effectiveness of a performer's embouchure or reed for the remainder of a performance. Embouchure suggestions for Group 6 fingerings also contradicted one another, with no discernable pattern related to the instrument's manufacturer or bassoonist's ability. The fingerings in Group 7 were not able to produce multiphonics with any recognizable predictability. Therefore, fingerings in Groups 6 and 7 were eliminated before Phase Three.

The remaining multiphonics were sorted into four categories. The first and second of these correspond with Groups 1 and 2 in Table 4. A third collection was the result of combining Groups 3, 4, and 5, while a fourth category was created for polyvalent fingerings (i.e., fingerings with more than one result).

---

[5] See Section 3 for a complete list, including modification of embouchure shape, placement, strength, and direction.

[6] These are approximate dynamic ranges.

1.3. Phase Three: Recording and Analysis

Phase Three involved recording and analyzing fingerings that remained after Phase Two. Every effort was made to maintain a consistent recording setup, in order to accurately determine pitch similarities. Mini condenser microphones were placed at the bell and over the left-hand toneholes on each instrument.[7] Microphones were set at the same level in each session, and bassoonists were asked to play at a *mf* dynamic.

Table 5. Bassoons in Phase Three

Instruments	Number
Heckel	3
Püchner	3
Fox	5
Mooseman	1
Yamaha	1

Table 6. Bassoonists in Phase Three

Bassoonists	Number
Professional	8
Young Professionals & Graduate Students	3
Undergraduate Students	1

To ensure limited familiarity with the embouchure manipulations required for each multiphonic, bassoonists did not have access to the fingerings before their Phase Two recording session. Bassoonists were asked to begin each multiphonic from a relaxed, neutral embouchure setting. If a fingering required manipulations, bassoonists took time to find the embouchure placement, then described it.[8] The embouchure setting was then compared to Phase Two suggestions, and other bassoonists' responses in Phase Three.

After the recording process was completed, tracks were mixed and bounced, then separated into three-second fragments.

1.4. Phase Four: Comparative Analysis and Selection of Pitch Content

Each recorded fragment was analyzed using an audio editing program, which contained a spectral analysis tool. The sonogram[9] created by this tool provided both the approximate pitch (closest semitone) and the exact frequency of each dynamic peak within the

---

[7] The mini condenser microphones were purchased from Bartlett Audio in North Carolina. These microphones were used for the entire study.

[8] For a full list of embouchure terminology, see Section 3.

[9] A visual representation of each acoustic sample presenting frequency in Hz on the X-axis and loudness in dB on the Y-axis.

4

recording. For example, if the loudest pitch in a file is 546.3 Hz, then the nearest semitone is C#5, whose exact frequency is 554.4 Hz.[10] However, this frequency is more accurately indentified as C#5.

In a two-step process, each pitch and exact frequency was documented and classified into three decibel ranges: -20+dB, -20.1 to -30dB, and -30.1 to -35dB.[11] The first step involved noting the approximate pitch (closest semitone) on staff paper and collecting the exact frequency. The exact frequency was then used to find the nearest eighth-tone. To compile the final pitch content of each fingering, it was necessary to view the results of this process as a simple collection.

Table 7 shows the multiphonic pitch content levels for all bassoonists able to play a multiphonic using fingering 120. To be included in the final pitch content, a frequency had to be produced on at least five bassoons. If, however, there were three or four identical frequencies, neighboring pitches were also used to determine a frequency's inclusion. For example, while there were only three bassoons that produced C#6, there were additional bassoons that produced pitches within a few eighth-tones. Contextually, this frequency warranted inclusion in the final pitch content of this fingering.

While the pitch content documented in Section 5 highlights the pitches that are most often present, in practice and performance the total frequency content will vary.

---

[10] Relative to A440

[11] It is important to note that while seemingly arbitrary, these ranges provide the basis for comparing multiphonic pitch content between bassoonists.

Table 7. Exact Frequencies for Multiphonic 120

Fingering	Bassoonist	Instrument	Decibel Range	Frequency (Hz)	Pitch (to nearest 8th tone)
120	Bassoon G	Fox	-30.1 to -35	1300.3	D♯ 6
120	Bassoon J	Fox	-30.1 to -35	1286.5	D♯ 6
120	Bassoon B	Püchner	-30.1 to -35	1283.8	D♯ 6
120	Bassoon E	Fox	-30.1 to -35	1119.6	C♯ 6
120	Bassoon I	Püchner	-30.1 to -35	1119.6	C♯ 6
120	Bassoon A	Mooseman	-20.1 to -30	1117.1	C♯ 6
120	Bassoon D	Heckel	-30.1 to -35	1103.7	C♯ 6
120	Bassoon G	Fox	-20.1 to -30	1100.7	C♯ 6
120	Bassoon D	Heckel	-30.1 to -35	1044.3	C 6
120	Bassoon A	Mooseman	-30.1 to -35	918.0	A♯ 5
120	Bassoon A	Mooseman	-20.1 to -30	877.5	A 5
120	Bassoon F	Heckel	-20.1 to -30	874.4	A 5
120	Bassoon H	Püchner	-30.1 to -35	872.1	G♯ 5
120	Bassoon G	Fox	-20.1 to -30	866.8	G♯ 5
120	Bassoon D	Heckel	-20.1 to -30	858.6	G♯ 5
120	Bassoon J	Fox	-30.1 to -35	858.5	G♯ 5
120	Bassoon B	Püchner	-20.1 to -30	855.8	G♯ 5
120	Bassoon B	Püchner	-30.1 to -35	672.8	E♯ 5
120	Bassoon J	Fox	-30.1 to -35	667.4	E♯ 5
120	Bassoon G	Fox	-20.1 to -30	667.3	E♯ 5
120	Bassoon J	Fox	-30.1 to -35	619.0	D♯ 5
120	Bassoon D	Heckel	-20.1 to -30	616.7	D♯ 5
120	Bassoon B	Püchner	-20.1 to -30	610.9	D♯ 5
120	Bassoon B	Püchner	-30.1 to -35	608.2	D♯ 5
120	Bassoon F	Heckel	-20.1 to -30	438.9	A 4
120	Bassoon A	Mooseman	-20.1 to -30	438.7	A 4
120	Bassoon H	Püchner	-30.1 to -35	436.0	G♯ 4
120	Bassoon E	Fox	-20.1 to -30	436.0	G♯ 4
120	Bassoon I	Püchner	-20.1 to -30	436.0	G♯ 4
120	Bassoon G	Fox	-20 +	433.4	G♯ 4
120	Bassoon D	Heckel	-20 +	430.9	G♯ 4
120	Bassoon J	Fox	-20.1 to -30	427.9	G♯ 4
120	Bassoon C	Yamaha	-20.1 to -30	425.2	G♯ 4
120	Bassoon D	Heckel	-30.1 to -35	371.4	F♯ 4
120	Bassoon D	Heckel	-20.1 to -30	245.2	B 3
120	Bassoon B	Püchner	-30.1 to -35	244.9	A♯ 3
120	Bassoon A	Mooseman	-30.1 to -35	239.6	A♯ 3
120	Bassoon D	Heckel	-30.1 to -35	185.7	F♯ 3

2. Monovalent and Polyvalent Fingerings

There are two categories of fingerings on the bassoon: monovalent and polyvalent.[1] Monovalent fingerings produce a single result, either a standard tone or a multiphonic. Many of the standard fingerings on the bassoon are monovalent fingerings. Polyvalent fingerings, on the other hand, may produce up to three results: a standard tone, a multiphonic, or a harmonic. Figure 1 provides an illustration of these relationships.

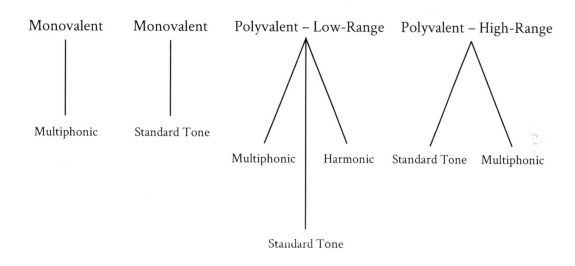

Figure 1. Monovalent and Polyvalent Fingering Results

2.1. Monovalent Fingerings

Each time a monovalent fingering is used it will produce the same results.[2] Example 1a includes a standard fingering and its pitch result. This pitch will occur every time this fingering is used. Similarly, the fingering in Example 1b will produce the same multiphonic each time it is used. Monovalent fingerings for standard tones are typically found between F2 and E-flat 4. Monovalent multiphonic fingerings are often related to

---

[1] These terms have not been used frequently since they were first published in Reginald Smith Brindle's translation of Bruno Bartolozzi's *New Sounds for Woodwind*; however, they do provide an accurate description of the acoustic possibilities that result from a single fingering.

[2] Jamie Leigh Sampson, "Polyvalent Fingerings for the Bassoon: An Introduction," *The Double Reed* 37, no. 1 (2014): 134–142.

standard fingerings. Example 1b is closely related to both the B-flat 2 and the E-flat 2 fingerings.

Example 1a   **Example 1b**

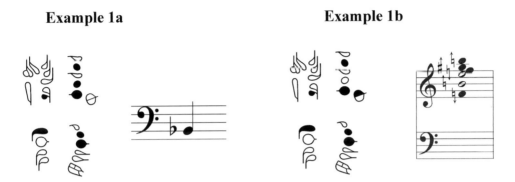

Multiphonic Group One, Two, and Three in Section 5 of this book contain monovalent fingerings. "The acoustic results of these fingerings are capable of being performed with a wide dynamic spectrum and with great sensitivity to articulation, though the reliability of monovalent fingerings does not preclude the need to place each multiphonic with a specific embouchure setting—just as you would any single tone throughout the bassoon's range."[3] Composers should note that it is possible to play a passage of monovalent multiphonics, either slurred or articulated, as quickly as standard tones. The adjusted embouchure placement for each multiphonic is no different than the changes required to perform a monophonic passage.

The three groups of monovalent multiphonics included in this text are categorized by ease of production and dynamic range. Group One multiphonics are the easiest to produce, and have the widest dynamic spectrum. Group Two multiphonics require some embouchure manipulation, but still have a relatively wide dynamic range. Group Three multiphonics responded on at least half of the instruments tested; however, they may offer a more restricted dynamic range as compared with Group One and Two.

2.2. Polyvalent Fingerings

Group Four fingerings are all polyvalent. They relate to standard pitches in two distinct ranges on the bassoon. The low-range fingerings (see Example 2) will produce a standard tone, harmonic, or multiphonic (a collection of harmonics), while the high-range fingerings (see Example 3) produce either a standard tone or a multiphonic. The use of

---

[3] Jamie Leigh Sampson, "Polyvalent Fingerings for the Bassoon: An Introduction," *The Double Reed* 37, no. 1 (2014): 134–142.

the E-flat and D-flat keys disrupts the production of multiphonics in both the high and low ranges. It is possible for some bassoonists to sustain a multiphonic or harmonic using the D-flat 2, E-flat 2, and B-flat 4 fingerings; however, fewer than four bassoonists in this study were able to do so.

Example 2   **Example 3**

The different results for each polyvalent fingering are due to modified embouchure placement and pressure. In his article "Response Issues on the Bassoon: Cracking Low Notes, Cracking High Notes, Bocal Flex – Voicing – Foghorn Effect," Michael Burns describes a technique to prevent cracking articulation in the polyvalent ranges.[4] He calls this technique Bocal Flex.[5] Cracked articulations occur when the embouchure is set for a higher register while playing a low-range polyvalent fingering, or vice versa. The result is a momentary multiphonic or harmonic, followed by the intended standard tone.

2.3. Isolating Polyvalent Results

Bassoonists who learn the mechanics behind the mistakes they make in embouchure placement, and learn to control both the desired result (usually the standard pitch associated with the fingering) and their accidental discovery (a harmonic or multiphonic), will be able to diagnose problems in the practice room quickly. Learning the point at which a single tone breaks into a multiphonic is crucial for tone production in the polyvalent ranges; however, the ability to isolate and sustain each result is equally important.

---

[4] Michael Burns, "Response Issues on the Bassoon: Cracking Low Notes, Cracking High Notes, Bocal Flex – Voicing – Foghorn Effect," *The Double Reed* 30, no. 4 (2007): 71–75.

[5] Burn's bocal flex technique can be used to reduce cracked articulations, as well as isolate multiphonics and harmonics. By thoroughly ingraining the embouchure settings to execute multiphonics and harmonics, bassoonists can improve their standard technique as well as these contemporary techniques.

2.3.1. Low-Range

The multiphonics and harmonics produced by low-range polyvalent fingerings are overtones of the pitches in Example 2. Three potential sonic results for the B♭1 fingering are presented in Example 4.

Example 4

To produce a multiphonic or harmonic, it is necessary to maintain a steady airflow and an open embouchure while lifting the chin up. The fundamental will break into a multiphonic or harmonic.

2.3.2. High-Range

The multiphonics produced by high-range polyvalent fingerings are sometimes referred to as "subharmonics"[6] of the pitches in Example 3. Two sonic results for the B4 fingering are presented in Example 5.

Example 5

[6] Michael Burns, "Response Issues on the Bassoon: Cracking Low Notes, Cracking High Notes, Bocal Flex – Voicing – Foghorn Effect," *The Double Reed* 30, no. 4 (2007): 71–75.

To produce a multiphonic from a high-range polyvalent fingering, it is necessary to maintain a steady airflow and an open embouchure while lowering the chin. The standard pitch will break into a multiphonic.

3. Embouchure Terminology

The terminology used to describe embouchure changes can differ from one school of teaching to the next. This section features definitions of all embouchure suggestions included in Section 5. Embouchure placement and voicing are as important to multiphonic production as they are to the production of standard tones. When practicing a passage that incorporates multiphonics, it is necessary to experiment with embouchure settings that will produce each multiphonic's pitch content with the greatest dynamic flexibility. Previous methods of embouchure notation, which use a small symbol to represent pressure and placement on the reed, are not capable of conveying the multidimensional manipulations that can assist your production of multiphonics. For this reason, a more robust system is used here to convey salient information.

3.1. Embouchure Placement

Figure 2 shows the areas of the reed where the embouchure can be placed. At the first wire is rarely needed. When stated, however, the embouchure should be placed on the bark just behind the collar, with lips touching the first wire.

At the Tip

Closer to the Tip

Middle of the Reed

Back of the Reed

At the Collar
At the First Wire

Figure 2

3.2. Embouchure Shape

Bassoonists are always encouraged to play with a round embouchure; however, when using different types of pressure (see Section 3.3.1) it is sometimes necessary to use an elliptical embouchure.

> **Round**: supported from all directions equally, with corners pulled in. This is typically the bassoonist's standard embouchure.
>
> **Elliptical**: supported from all directions with slightly relaxed corners.

3.3. Pressure on the Blades

Pressure can either be added to a single blade or both blades of the reed, with varying degrees of force. As described in Section 2.3, adding pressure to a single blade while maintaining an open embouchure is required for producing Group Four multiphonics. To accomplish this it is necessary to experiment with the full range of your embouchure's capabilities.

3.3.1. Direction

Pressure can be added to one or both blades of the reed by moving the head, or closing the jaw.

Even Pressure: add pressure to both blades with a round embouchure by closing the jaw.

Vertical Pressure: add pressure to both blades with an elliptical embouchure by closing the jaw.

Lowered Jaw: open the jaw while maintaining the position of the upper lip.

Head Tilted: tilt either to the right or left around the reed to offset pressure and encourage instability. This is particularly useful for high-range polyvalent fingerings, but is also used for some monovalent multiphonics. Typically, pressure on the blades is symmetrical, but by changing the embouchure placement, embouchure pressure is offset. This causes instability, allowing a standard tone to break into a multiphonic.

Bocal Flex:[1] change the inflexion of the bocal by slightly lifting or lowering the chin.

Bocal Flex Up: tilt the head up while maintaining an open embouchure; this will add pressure to the bottom blade of the reed.

Bocal Flex Down: tilt the head down while maintaining an open embouchure; this will add pressure to the top blade of the reed.

3.3.2. Force

The degree of force depends on the firmness of the lip muscles around the reed.

Loose pressure: relax muscles as much as possible.

Light Pressure: flex muscles slightly.

Firm embouchure: use medium pressure (similar to mid-range embouchure).

Tight Pressure: use tightest embouchure setting (similar to high-range embouchure).

---

[1] Michael Burns, "Response Issues on the Bassoon: Cracking Low Notes, Cracking High Notes, Bocal Flex – Voicing – Foghorn Effect," *The Double Reed* 30, no. 4 (2007): 71–75.

Biting:[2] add pressure from the teeth with firm embouchure muscles. (Used infrequently.)

3.4. Voicing

It is necessary to use a combination of throat aperture manipulation and tongue placement, otherwise known as **voicing**, to direct airflow through the reed.

3.4.1. Throat Aperture

Aperture, a term borrowed from photography, refers to the relative diameter of the throat.

> **Open**: often used in the lowest range when executing standard tones.
> **Restricted**: narrower, often used when directing a more focused air column (see Section 3.5).

3.4.2. Tongue Placement

Tongue placement can either refer to a specific vowel sound or a general high or low placement. For the most part, **high tongue placement** or **low tongue placement** is used in the embouchure suggestions in Section 3. However, using a more specific placement may be necessary for some fingerings. It is useful to experiment with several open vowels while sustaining a multiphonic.

3.4.3. Pre-existing Settings

Many monovalent multiphonic fingerings call for embouchure settings that are familiar to most bassoonists. Fingerings either call for a **low-range embouchure setting** or a **high-range embouchure setting**. Sometimes the bassoonists who tested multiphonic fingerings referenced a pitch, for example E4 or E5, to identify a specific, familiar setting.

3.5. Special Indications

There are several multiphonics which use one of the following settings; both require

---

[2] Composers, please note that if a bassoonist indicates they must bite the reed to perform a particular multiphonic, extended technique, or pitch in the extremely high range, it should only be used once or twice. Biting is not only tiring, but it can significantly affect the reed's response capability in other ranges of the instrument for the remainder of a performance.

experimentation.

Narrow embouchure range: requires placement with limited flexibility to produce a multiphonic.

Focused embouchure: requires precise placement with no flexibility; often corresponds with fingerings that only have one associated dynamic level.

4. Notation

The notation of contemporary techniques is a continuously evolving and fluid language. Several styles of multiphonic notation have developed since they were first introduced in the 1950s. Choosing a particular style may be specific to one score, a section within a score, or a composer's entire oeuvre. Each of the four notation styles presented in this section have benefits and drawbacks.

4.1. Full Pitch Notation

Figure 3. Full Pitch Notation

Full Pitch Notation is one of the most common styles of multiphonic notation. It was introduced in early resources, including Bartolozzi's *New Sounds for Woodwind*, and used in many historic compositions that included multiphonics. Figure 3 illustrates this style, which includes the full pitch content in the staff and a pictorial fingering above. There are a few variations of this notation. In some scores a symbol for embouchure settings is added, or the pictorial fingering is removed. Spacing staves around a pictorial fingering can be cumbersome, but when using full pitch notation it is always preferable to include it.

The primary benefit of this notation style is that performers are able to see the pitches they are expected to produce. In solo works, performers gain a clear impression of density and tension over the course of the composition. In chamber music, this style facilitates ensemble tuning. In Example 6, the flute player sustains a pitch contained within the bassoonist's multiphonic.[1]

Example 6

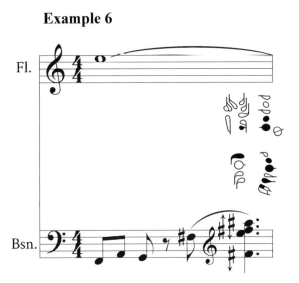

One of the primary drawbacks to this notation is the amount of space taken by the pictorial fingering. Not only does it cost more in resources to have blank space between the staves, it can leave a score looking uneven. If you choose not to include pictorial fingerings above the staff, they must be included in preface materials, or as an insert that can be placed next to the score on the music stand.

4.2. Abbreviated Pitch Notation

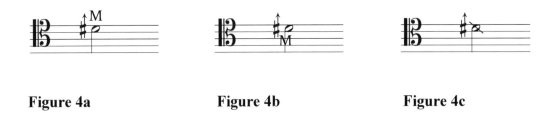

Figure 4a　　　　　　　**Figure 4b**　　　　　　　**Figure 4c**

A single notehead and symbol are used to represent the most prominent pitch in Abbreviated Pitch Notation. A symbol may be placed over the stem, over the notehead, or through the notehead (see Figures 4a, 4b, and 4c). A variation of this notation style includes a pictorial fingering above the notehead. Several symbols found in recent scores

[1] N.B. If the notated pitches are not present on a particular instrument, bassoonists can seek fingerings with a pitch content closely related to those in the score.

are included in Example 7.

Example 7

Abbreviated Pitch Notation is beneficial when Full Pitch Notation is too cumbersome, for example in repetitive passages with dense pitch content (see Example 8a and 8b). It provides some pitch content while leaving the score uncluttered.

Example 8a

Example 8b

The primary weakness of this notation style is that it neither gives the full pitch content, nor the full fingering.

4.3. Full Fingering Notation

Figure 5

Full Fingering Notation is particularly useful in quick and/or repetitive passages, since the noteheads are associated with the fingerings bassoonists already recognize, not their resulting pitches. Donald Christlieb provided a similar notation in *Pictoral Fingerings for Bassoon* (1966), as did Leslie Ross on her website. The fingerings presented in Christlieb's books are, for the most part, standard pitches with one tonehole opened; there are very few instances of changes that involve keys. For that reason, his notation used solid noteheads to indicate which finger was lifted.

The notation suggestions in Section 5 are based upon standard fingerings. In Example 9a, F2 is the fundamental fingering from which a multiphonic is constructed. In Example 9b, to indicate an open key or tonehole (one that would be otherwise depressed) an open diamond-notehead is placed on the staff corresponding to the lifted key (see Table 8). In Example 9c, to indicate a depressed key or tonehole (one that would be otherwise lifted) a solid diamond-notehead is placed on the staff corresponding to the depressed key.

Example 9a	**Example 9b**	**Example 9c**

Table 8 shows the pitch position corresponding to each key and tonehole for Full Fingering Notation. Example 10 is a side-by-side comparison of the Full Fingering Notation and Full Pitch Notation for Multiphonic 72.

Example 10

Full Fingering Notation   Full Pitch Notation

This style of notation shows performers the full fingering without altering stave spacing. There are two disadvantages to Full Fingering Notation. It is difficult to read more than five changes to the original fingering,[2] and this notation gives no indication of pitch content.

---

[2] The multiphonic tables in Section 5 only include notation suggestions for fingerings with five or fewer changes.

Table 8. Full Fingering Notation Key

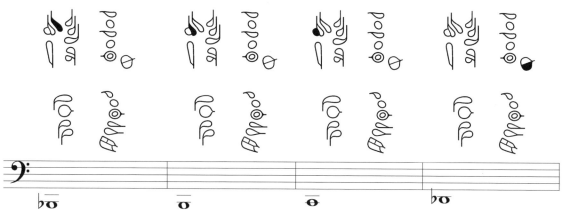

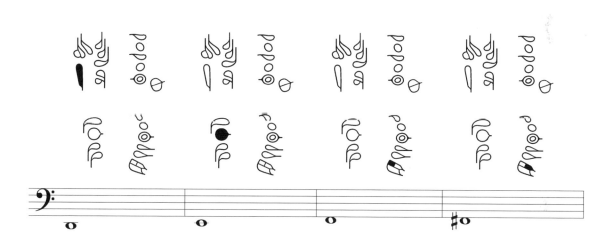

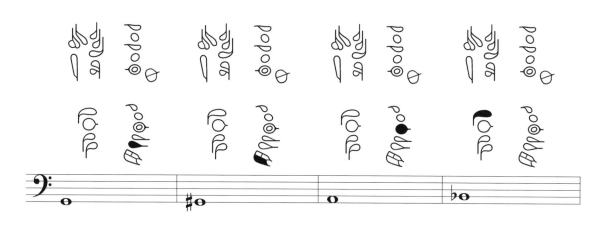

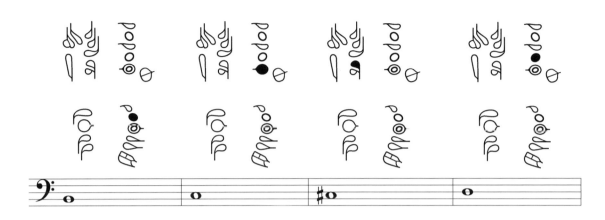

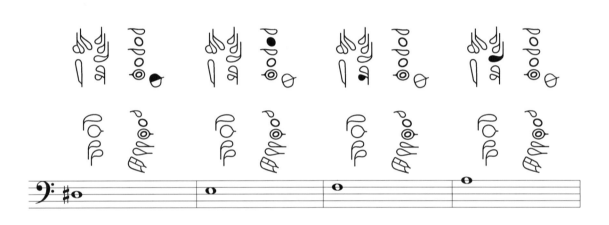

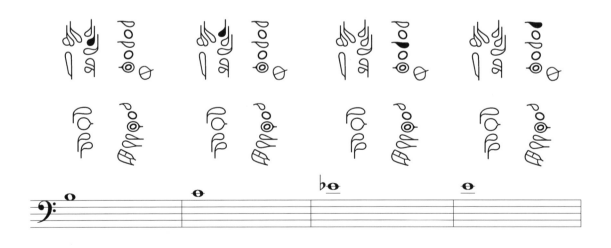

4.4. Abbreviated Fingering Notation

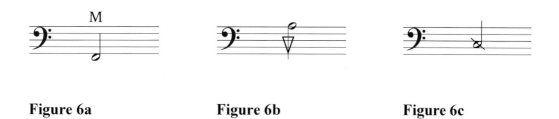

Figure 6a **Figure 6b** **Figure 6c**

Abbreviated Fingering Notation uses a single notehead placed according to the standard tone that is most closely related to the multiphonic fingering, with a symbol over the stem, over the notehead, or through the notehead. Sofia Gubaidulina (b. 1931) used Abbreviated Fingering Notation in her *Concerto for Bassoon and Low Strings*,[3] as well as her nonet *Hommage à T.S. Eliot*.[4] In these two scores she places an isosceles triangle under the notehead, similar to Figure 6b, and a pictorial fingering above the stave. Several symbols found in recent scores are included in Example 7 in Section 4.2.

Having the same benefits associated with Abbreviated Pitch Notation, Abbreviated Fingering Notation presents the best solution for polyvalent fingerings. It gives the full fingering and, especially when used with Gubaidulina's isosceles triangle, a visual representation for the embouchure manipulation.

4.5. Selecting Multiphonic Notation

When selecting a notation style for a new work, there are many factors to consider. Aside from personal or performer preference, there is a strong case for selecting one style over another. Monovalent multiphonics are easier to read when presented in Full Fingering Notation. If the monovalent fingering does not have a full fingering suggestion, it is best to use either the Full Pitch Notation or the Abbreviated Fingering Notation. Both should be used in conjunction with pictorial fingerings above the staff.

Abbreviated Fingering Notation is highly recommended for all polyvalent fingerings. Using the isosceles triangle symbol works well. In addition to showing the full fingering, the triangle is an accurate depiction of the bocal flex technique.

---

[3] Sofia Gubaidulina, *Concerto for Bassoon and Low Strings* (Hamburg: H. Sikorski, 1975).

[4] Sofia Gubaidulina, *Hommage à T.S. Eliot* (Hamburg: H. Sikorski, 1987).

Abbreviated Pitch Notation should be used as a last resort. It shows neither the full fingering nor the full pitch content. The three other styles give a more complete picture of the desired result.

If Abbreviated Pitch Notation or either of the fingering notations are used within the score, Full Pitch Notation should be included in the preface materials.

5. Multiphonics

The multiphonics in this section are formatted to allow readers easy access to all pertinent information associated with each fingering. The content block for Fingering 91 illustrates this formatting, and includes most of the elements found within all other multiphonic content blocks (see Example 11). In addition to the pictorial representation of fingering, content blocks also include the Full Fingering Notation,[1] pitch content, embouchure notes, information for composers, and reliable dynamic range. The pitch content is presented in three dynamic levels, with pitches in the left-most column being louder than those to the right.[2] The dynamic range for each fingering is indicated within brackets. Many content blocks also include space for readers to make personal notes about each multiphonic.

Example 11

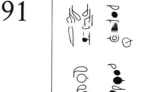

91

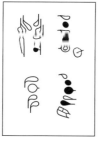

Notation

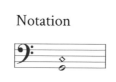

Pitch Content

Embouchure Suggestions
• Focused Embouchure

For Composers
• Individual bassoonists may be limited to a single dynamic

Dynamic Range

pp–p [mp–mf–f] ff

---

[1] Full Fingering Notation was not included for multiphonics that require more than five changes to the fundamental fingering (see Section 4.3).

[2] See Section 1.4 for a full description of pitch content selection.

5.1. Group One: Monovalent Multiphonics

Group One multiphonics are the easiest to produce, require the fewest embouchure changes, and have the widest dynamic ranges. A novice with less than one year of experience was able to produce all Group One multiphonics.

3

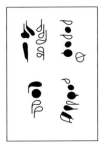

Notation

Pitch Content

Dynamic Range

$\left[\; pp - p - mp - mf - f \;\right] ff$

4

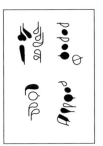

Notation

Pitch Content

Dynamic Range

$pp \left[\; p - mp - mf - f - ff \;\right]$

5

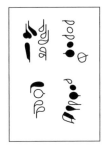

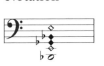

Notation

Pitch Content

Dynamic Range

$\left[\; pp - p - mp - mf - f \;\right] ff$

28

6

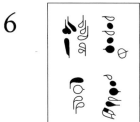

Notation

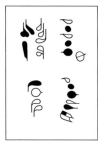

Pitch Content

Dynamic Range

$pp\left[\,p-mp-mf-f\,\right]ff$

7

Notation

Pitch Content

Dynamic Range

$\left[\,pp-p-mp-mf-f\,\right]ff$

8

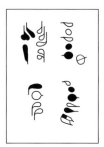

Notation

Pitch Content

Dynamic Range

$pp\left[\,p-mp-mf-f-ff\,\right]$

9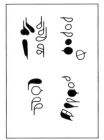

Pitch Content

Dynamic Range

$$\left[\, pp - p - mp - mf - f - ff \,\right]$$

10

Pitch Content

Dynamic Range

$$\left[\, pp - p - mp - mf - f - ff \,\right]$$

11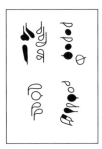

Notation

Pitch Content

Dynamic Range

$$pp \left[\, p - mp - mf - f - ff \,\right]$$

12

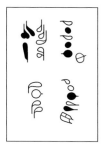

Pitch Content

Notation

Dynamic Range

$\left[\,\boldsymbol{pp}-\boldsymbol{p}-\boldsymbol{mp}-\boldsymbol{mf}-\boldsymbol{f}-\boldsymbol{ff}\,\right]$

13

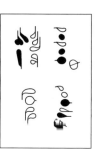

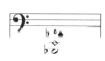

Pitch Content

Notation

Dynamic Range

$\boldsymbol{pp}\left[\,\boldsymbol{p}-\boldsymbol{mp}-\boldsymbol{mf}-\boldsymbol{f}\,\right]\boldsymbol{ff}$

14

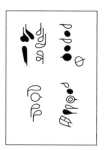

Pitch Content

Notation

Dynamic Range

$\boldsymbol{pp}\left[\,\boldsymbol{p}-\boldsymbol{mp}-\boldsymbol{mf}-\boldsymbol{f}\,\right]\boldsymbol{ff}$

15

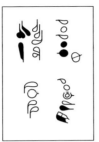

Pitch Content

Dynamic Range

$$pp\left[\,p-mp-mf-f\,\right]ff$$

16

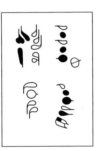

Notation

Pitch Content

Dynamic Range

$$\left[\,pp-p-mp-mf-f-ff\,\right]$$

17

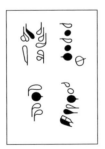

Pitch Content

Dynamic Range

$$pp\left[\,p-mp-mf-f-ff\,\right]$$

18

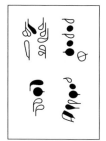

Pitch Content

Dynamic Range

$pp\left[\,p-mp-mf-f-ff\,\right]$

19

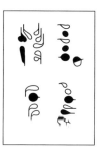

Notation

Pitch Content

Dynamic Range

$pp\left[\,p-mp-mf-f-ff\,\right]$

20

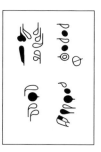

Notation

Pitch Content

Dynamic Range

$\left[\,pp-p-mp-mf-f\,\right]ff$

21

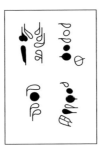

Pitch Content

Notation

Dynamic Range

$pp\left[\,p-mp-mf-f\,\right]ff$

22

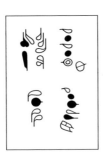

Pitch Content

Notation

Dynamic Range

$\left[\,pp-p-mp-mf-f-ff\,\right]$

23

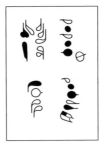

Pitch Content

Notation

Dynamic Range

$pp\left[\,p-mp-mf-f\,\right]ff$

24

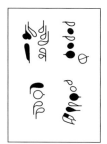

Pitch Content

Notation

Dynamic Range

$pp\,[\,p-mp-mf-f\,]\,ff$

25

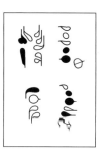

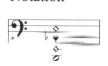

Pitch Content

Notation

Dynamic Range

$pp\,[\,p-mp-mf-f\,]\,ff$

26

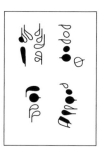

Pitch Content

Notation

Dynamic Range

$pp\,[\,p-mp-mf-f\,]\,ff$

27

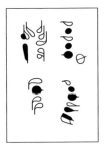

Pitch Content

Notation

Dynamic Range

$pp\left[\,p-mp-mf-f\,\right]ff$

28

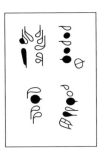

Pitch Content

Notation

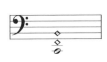

Dynamic Range

$\left[\,pp-p-mp-mf-f-ff\,\right]$

29

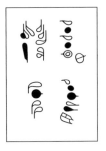

Pitch Content

Notation

Dynamic Range

$\left[\,pp-p-mp-mf-f-ff\,\right]$

30

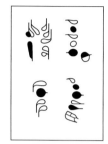

Pitch Content

Notation

Dynamic Range

$\left[\, pp - p - mp - mf - f - ff \,\right]$

31

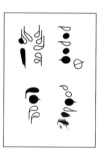

Pitch Content

Notation

Dynamic Range

$\left[\, pp - p - mp - mf - f \,\right] ff$

32

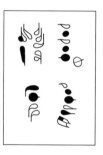

Pitch Content

Notation

Embouchure Suggestions
- Firm Embouchure
- Back of the Reed

Dynamic Range

$pp \left[\, p - mp - mf - f \,\right] ff$

33

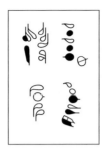

Pitch Content

Notation

Dynamic Range

$pp\left[p-mp-mf-f-ff\right]$

34

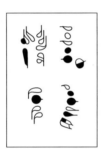 

Pitch Content

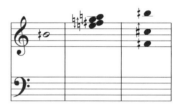

Notation

Dynamic Range

$\left[pp-p-mp-mf-f-ff\right]$

35

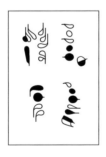 

Pitch Content

Notation

Dynamic Range

$\left[pp-p-mp-mf-f\right]ff$

36

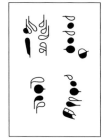

Notation

Pitch Content

Embouchure Suggestions:
• Bocal Flex Up

Dynamic Range

$pp\left[\,p-mp-mf-f\,\right]ff$

37

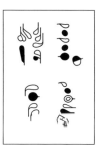

Notation

Pitch Content

Dynamic Range

$pp\left[\,p-mp-mf-f-ff\,\right]$

38

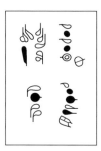

Notation

Pitch Content

Dynamic Range

$\left[\,pp-p-mp-mf-f-ff\,\right]$

39

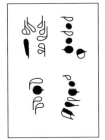

Notation

Pitch Content

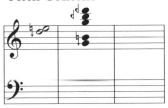

Dynamic Range

$pp\left[\,p-mp-mf-f\,\right]ff$

40

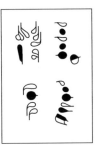

Notation

Pitch Content

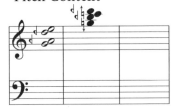

Dynamic Range

$pp\left[\,p-mp-mf-f\,\right]ff$

41

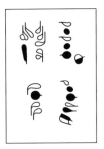

Notation

Pitch Content

Dynamic Range

$pp\left[\,p-mp-mf-f\,\right]ff$

42

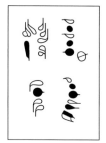

Notation

Pitch Content

Dynamic Range

$pp\left[\,p-mp-mf-f\,\right]ff$

43

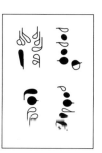

Notation

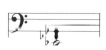

Pitch Content

Dynamic Range

$pp\left[\,p-mp-mf-f\,\right]ff$

44

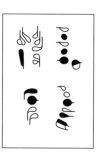

Notation

Pitch Content

Dynamic Range

$pp\left[\,p-mp-mf-f\,\right]ff$

45

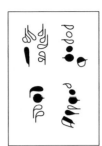

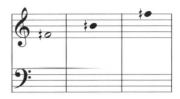

Pitch Content

Notation

Dynamic Range

$\left[\, pp - p - mp - mf - f \,\right] f\!f$

46

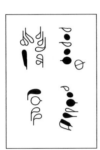

Pitch Content

Notation

Dynamic Range

$pp \left[\, p - mp - mf - f \,\right] f\!f$

47

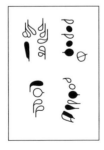

Pitch Content

Notation

Dynamic Range

$pp \left[\, p - mp - mf - f \,\right] f\!f$

48

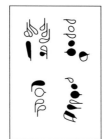

Pitch Content

Notation

Dynamic Range

$\left[\,\mathit{pp} - \mathit{p} - \mathit{mp} - \mathit{mf} - \mathit{f} - \mathit{ff}\,\right]$

49

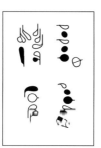

Pitch Content

Notation

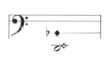

Dynamic Range

$\left[\,\mathit{pp} - \mathit{p} - \mathit{mp} - \mathit{mf} - \mathit{f} - \mathit{ff}\,\right]$

50

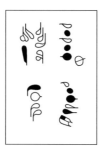

Pitch Content

Notation

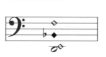

Dynamic Range

$\mathit{pp}\left[\,\mathit{p} - \mathit{mp} - \mathit{mf} - \mathit{f}\,\right]\mathit{ff}$

51

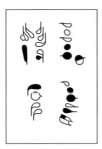

Pitch Content

Notation

Dynamic Range

$pp\left[\,p-mp-mf-f\,\right]ff$

52

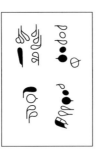

Pitch Content

Notation

Dynamic Range

$pp\left[\,p-mp-mf-f\,\right]ff$

53

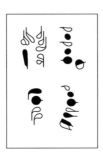

Pitch Content

Notation

Dynamic Range

$pp-p\left[\,mp-mf-f-ff\,\right]$

54

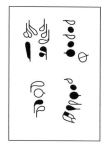

Notation

Pitch Content

Dynamic Range

$\left[\,\boldsymbol{pp}-\boldsymbol{p}-\boldsymbol{mp}-\boldsymbol{mf}-\boldsymbol{f}-\boldsymbol{ff}\,\right]$

55

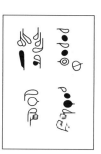

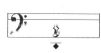

Notation

Pitch Content

Dynamic Range

$\boldsymbol{pp}\left[\,\boldsymbol{p}-\boldsymbol{mp}-\boldsymbol{mf}-\boldsymbol{f}-\boldsymbol{ff}\,\right]$

56

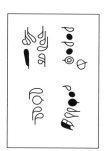

Notation

Pitch Content

Dynamic Range

$\boldsymbol{pp}\left[\,\boldsymbol{p}-\boldsymbol{mp}-\boldsymbol{mf}-\boldsymbol{f}-\boldsymbol{ff}\,\right]$

57

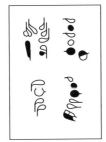

Pitch Content

Embouchure Suggestions:
- Firm Embouchure

Dynamic Range

$$\left[\, \boldsymbol{pp} - \boldsymbol{p} - \boldsymbol{mp} - \boldsymbol{mf} - \boldsymbol{f} - \boldsymbol{ff} \,\right]$$

58

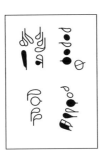

Notation

Pitch Content

Dynamic Range

$$\left[\, \boldsymbol{pp} - \boldsymbol{p} - \boldsymbol{mp} - \boldsymbol{mf} - \boldsymbol{f} - \boldsymbol{ff} \,\right]$$

59

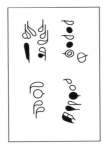

Pitch Content

Embouchure Suggestions:
- Firm Embouchure

Dynamic Range

$$\boldsymbol{pp}\left[\, \boldsymbol{p} - \boldsymbol{mp} - \boldsymbol{mf} - \boldsymbol{f} - \boldsymbol{ff} \,\right]$$

60

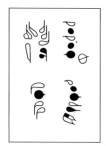

Notation

Pitch Content

Dynamic Range

$pp\left[\,p-mp-mf\,\right]f-ff$

61

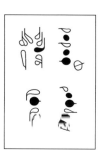

Notation

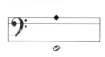

Pitch Content

Dynamic Range

$\left[\,pp-p-mp-mf-f\,\right]ff$

62

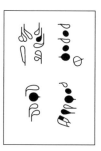

Notation

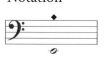

Pitch Content

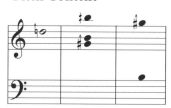

Embouchure Suggestions:
  • Loose Embouchure, At the Tip
  • Firmer Embouchure, Back of the Reed

Dynamic Range

$pp\left[\,p-mp-mf-f\,\right]ff$

63

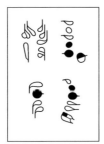

Notation

Pitch Content

Dynamic Range

$[\,pp\!-\!p\!-\!mp\!-\!mf\!-\!f\!-\!ff\,]$

64

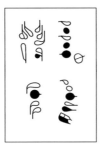

Notation

Pitch Content

Dynamic Range

$[\,pp\!-\!p\!-\!mp\!-\!mf\!-\!f\!-\!ff\,]$

65

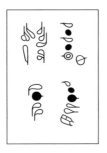

Notation

Pitch Content

Dynamic Range

$pp\,[\,p\!-\!mp\!-\!mf\!-\!f\!-\!ff\,]$

66

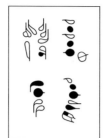

Notation

Pitch Content

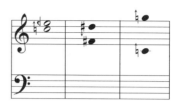

Dynamic Range

$\left[\, pp - p - mp - mf - f - ff \,\right]$

67

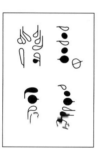

Notation

Pitch Content

Dynamic Range

$\left[\, pp - p - mp - mf - f \,\right] ff$

68

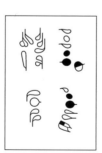

Notation

Pitch Content

Dynamic Range

$pp \left[\, p - mp - mf - f - ff \,\right]$

69

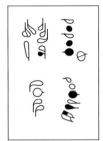

Pitch Content

Notation

Dynamic Range

$pp\left[\,p-mp-mf-f\,\right]ff$

70

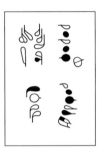

Pitch Content

Notation

Dynamic Range

$\left[\,pp-p-mp-mf-f-ff\,\right]$

71

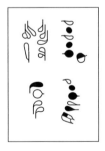

Pitch Content

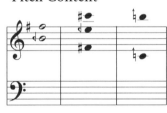

Notation

Dynamic Range

$\left[\,pp-p-mp-mf-f-ff\,\right]$

72

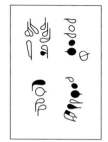

Pitch Content

Notation

Dynamic Range

$pp\left[\,p\!-\!mp\!-\!mf\!-\!f\,\right]ff$

73

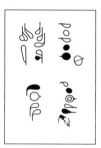

Pitch Content

Notation

Embouchure Suggestions
- Back of the Reed
- Bocal Flex Up
- Head Tilted

Dynamic Range

$\left[\,pp\!-\!p\!-\!mp\!-\!mf\!-\!f\,\right]ff$

74

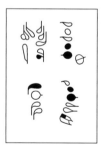

Pitch Content

Notation

Dynamic Range

$pp\left[\,p\!-\!mp\!-\!mf\!-\!f\!-\!ff\,\right]$

75

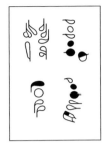

Pitch Content

Notation

Dynamic Range

$[\,pp-p-mp-mf-f\,]\,\boldsymbol{ff}$

76

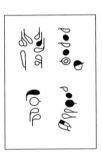

Pitch Content

Embouchure Suggestions
• Focused Embouchure
• Back of the Reed

Dynamic Range

$[\,pp-p-mp-mf-f\,]\,\boldsymbol{ff}$

77

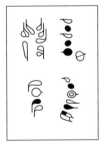

Pitch Content

Notation

Dynamic Range

$[\,pp-p-mp-mf-f-ff\,]$

78

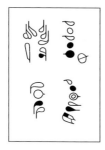

Notation

Pitch Content

Embouchure Suggestions
- Firm Embouchure
- Back of the Reed

Dynamic Range

$pp\!-\!p\left[\,mp\!-\!mf\!-\!f\,\right]\!ff$

79

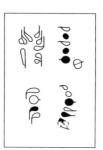

Notation

Pitch Content

Dynamic Range

$\left[\,pp\!-\!p\!-\!mp\!-\!mf\!-\!f\!-\!ff\,\right]$

80

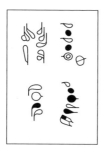

Notation

Pitch Content

Dynamic Range

$pp\!-\!p\left[\,mp\!-\!mf\,\right]\!f\!-\!ff$

81

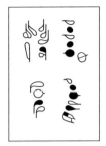

Notation

Pitch Content

Dynamic Range

pp–*p* [*mp*–*mf*–*f*] *ff*

82

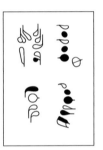

Notation

Pitch Content

Dynamic Range

[*pp*–*p*–*mp*–*mf*–*f*–*ff*]

83

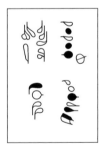

Notation

Pitch Content

Dynamic Range

pp [*p*–*mp*–*mf*–*f*] *ff*

84

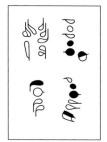

Notation

Pitch Content

Dynamic Range

$pp\left[\,p\!-\!mp\!-\!mf\!-\!f\!-\!ff\,\right]$

85

Notation

Pitch Content

Dynamic Range

$pp\left[\,p\!-\!mp\!-\!mf\!-\!f\,\right]ff$

86

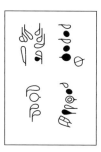

Notation

Pitch Content

Dynamic Range

$pp\left[\,p\!-\!mp\!-\!mf\!-\!f\,\right]ff$

87

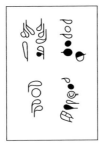

Pitch Content

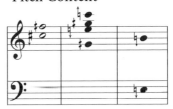

Notation

Dynamic Range

[*pp* – *p* – *mp* – *mf* – *f* – *ff*]

88

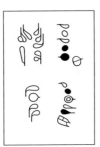

Pitch Content

Notation

Dynamic Range

[*pp* – *p* – *mp* – *mf* – *f*] *ff*

89

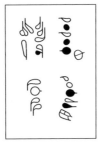

Pitch Content

Notation

Dynamic Range

[*pp* – *p* – *mp* – *mf* – *f* – *ff*]

90

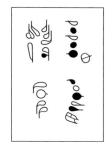

Notation

Pitch Content

Dynamic Range

$\left[\,pp-p-mp-mf-f\,\right]ff$

91

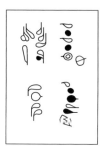

Notation

Pitch Content

Embouchure Suggestions
• Focused Embouchure

For Composers
• Individual bassoonists may be limited to a single dynamic

Dynamic Range

$pp-p\left[\,mp-mf-f\,\right]ff$

92

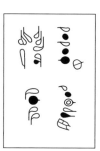

Notation

Pitch Content

Dynamic Range

$pp\left[\,p-mp-mf\,\right]f-ff$

93

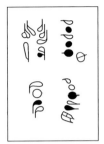

Notation

Pitch Content

Dynamic Range

$\left[\,pp-p-mp-mf-f\,\right]ff$

94

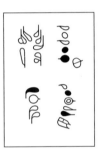

Notation

Pitch Content

Dynamic Range

$pp\left[\,p-mp-mf-f-ff\,\right]$

95

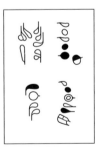

Notation

Pitch Content

Dynamic Range

$pp\left[\,p-mp-mf-f\,\right]ff$

96

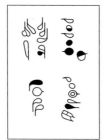

Pitch Content

Dynamic Range

$pp\,[\,p-mp-mf-f\,]\,ff$

97

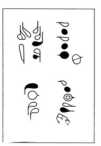

Notation

Pitch Content

Additional Notes
• Whisper Key Lock Required

Dynamic Range

$[\,pp-p-mp-mf\,]\,f-ff$

98

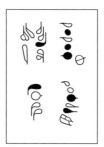

Pitch Content

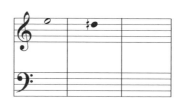

Dynamic Range

$[\,pp-p-mp-mf-f-ff\,]$

99

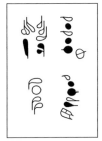

Notation

Pitch Content

Dynamic Range

$\left[\, pp - p - mp - mf - f - ff\,\right]$

100

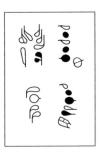

Notation

Pitch Content

Dynamic Range

$\left[\, pp - p - mp - mf - f\,\right] ff$

101

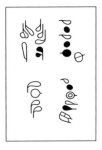

Notation

Pitch Content

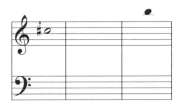

Dynamic Range

$pp \left[\, p - mp - mf - f\,\right] ff$

102

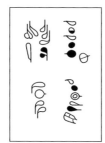

Pitch Content

Dynamic Range

$pp\left[p-mp-mf-f\right]ff$

103

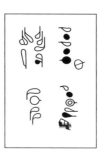

Notation

Pitch Content

Embouchure Suggestions
• Püchner's require a High-Range Embouchure

Dynamic Range

$\left[pp-p-mp-mf-f-ff\right]$

104

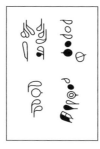

Notation

Pitch Content

Dynamic Range

$pp\left[p-mp-mf-f\right]ff$

105

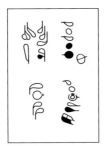

Notation

Pitch Content

Dynamic Range

$\left[\,pp-p-mp-mf-f-ff\,\right]$

106

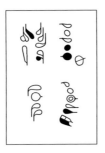

Notation

Pitch Content

Additional Notes
• Whisper Key Lock Required

Dynamic Range

$\left[\,pp-p-mp-mf-f-ff\,\right]$

107

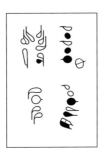

Notation

Pitch Content

Dynamic Range

$\left[\,pp-p-mp-mf-f-ff\,\right]$

108

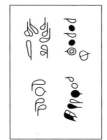

Notation

Pitch Content

Dynamic Range

$pp\left[\,p-mp-mf-f\,\right]ff$

109

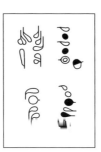

Notation

Pitch Content

Dynamic Range

$pp-p\left[\,mp-mf-f-ff\,\right]$

110

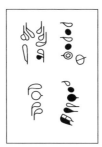

Notation

Pitch Content

Dynamic Range

$\left[\,pp-p-mp-mf-f-ff\,\right]$

111

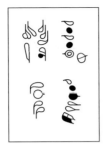

Notation

Pitch Content

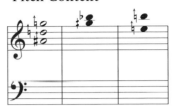

Dynamic Range

$\left[\, pp - p - mp - mf - f - ff \,\right]$

112

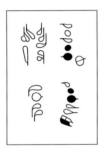

Notation

Pitch Content

Dynamic Range

$pp\left[\, p - mp - mf - f \,\right]ff$

113

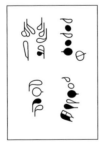

Notation

Pitch Content

Dynamic Range

$pp\left[\, p - mp - mf - f \,\right]ff$

114

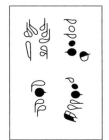

Notation

Pitch Content

Dynamic Range

$pp\left[\,p\!-\!mp\!-\!mf\!-\!f\!-\!ff\,\right]$

115

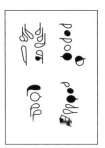

Notation

Pitch Content

Dynamic Range

$\left[\,pp\!-\!p\!-\!mp\!-\!mf\!-\!f\!-\!ff\,\right]$

116

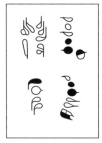

Notation

Pitch Content

Dynamic Range

$pp\left[\,p\!-\!mp\!-\!mf\!-\!f\!-\!ff\,\right]$

65

117

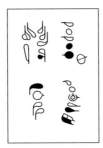

Pitch Content

Embouchure Suggestions
• Firm Embouchure

Dynamic Range

$\left[\,pp-p-mp-mf-f\,\right]f\!f$

118

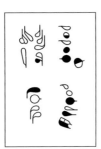

Pitch Content

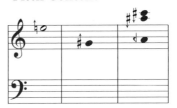

Dynamic Range

$pp\left[\,p-mp-mf-f-f\!f\,\right]$

119

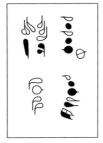

Notation

Pitch Content

Dynamic Range

$\left[\,pp-p-mp-mf-f-f\!f\,\right]$

120

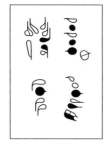

Notation

Pitch Content

Dynamic Range

$\left[\, pp - p - mp - mf - f \,\right] ff$

121

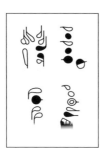

Pitch Content

Embouchure Suggestions
• Even Pressure, Back of the Reed

Dynamic Range

$\left[\, pp - p - mp - mf - f - ff \,\right]$

122

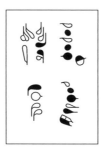

Notation

Pitch Content

Dynamic Range

$\left[\, pp - p - mp - mf - f - ff \,\right]$

123

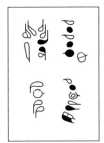

Notation

Pitch Content

Dynamic Range

$pp\left[\,p-mp-mf-f\,\right]ff$

124

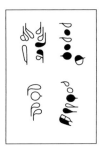

Notation

Pitch Content

Dynamic Range

$\left[\,pp-p-mp-mf-f-ff\,\right]$

125

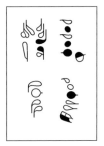

Notation

Pitch Content

Dynamic Range

$\left[\,pp-p-mp-mf-f-ff\,\right]$

126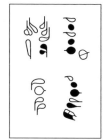

Notation

Pitch Content

Dynamic Range

$[\ \boldsymbol{pp} - \boldsymbol{p} - \boldsymbol{mp} - \boldsymbol{mf} - \boldsymbol{f} - \boldsymbol{ff}\ ]$

127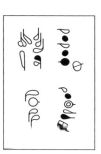

Notation

Pitch Content

Dynamic Range

$\boldsymbol{pp}\ [\ \boldsymbol{p} - \boldsymbol{mp} - \boldsymbol{mf} - \boldsymbol{f}\ ]\ \boldsymbol{ff}$

128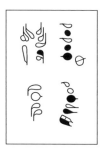

Notation

Pitch Content

Dynamic Range

$\boldsymbol{pp}\ [\ \boldsymbol{p} - \boldsymbol{mp} - \boldsymbol{mf} - \boldsymbol{f}\ ]\ \boldsymbol{ff}$

129

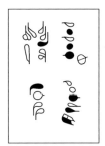

Notation

Pitch Content

Dynamic Range

$\left[\, pp - p - mp - mf - f\,\right] ff$

130

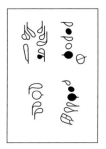

Notation

Pitch Content

Embouchure Suggestions
• Fox Bassoons – High-Range Embouchure

Dynamic Range

$pp \left[\, p - mp - mf - f\,\right] ff$

131

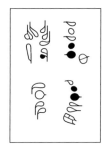

Notation

Pitch Content

Dynamic Range

$\left[\, pp - p - mp - mf - f - ff\,\right]$

132

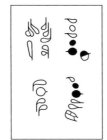

Notation

Pitch Content

Dynamic Range

$\left[\ \textit{pp} - \textit{p} - \textit{mp} - \textit{mf} - \textit{f} - \textit{ff}\ \right]$

133

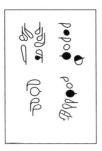

Notation

Pitch Content

Embouchure Suggestions
- Firm Embouchure
- Back of Reed

Dynamic Range

$\left[\ \textit{pp} - \textit{p} - \textit{mp} - \textit{mf} - \textit{f} - \textit{ff}\ \right]$

134

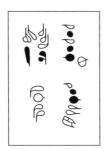

Notation

Pitch Content

Dynamic Range

$\left[\ \textit{pp} - \textit{p} - \textit{mp} - \textit{mf} - \textit{f} - \textit{ff}\ \right]$

135

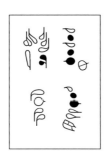

Pitch Content

Notation

Dynamic Range

$pp\left[\,p-mp-mf-f\,\right]ff$

136

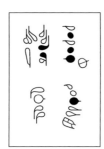

Pitch Content

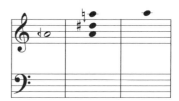

Notation

Dynamic Range

$pp\left[\,p-mp-mf-f\,\right]ff$

137

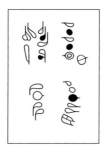

Pitch Content

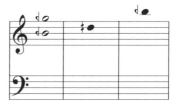

Notation

Additional Notes
• Whisper Key Lock Required

Dynamic Range

$pp\left[\,p-mp-mf-f\,\right]ff$

138

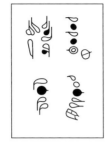

Notation

Pitch Content

Additional Notes
- Whisper Key Lock Required

Dynamic Range

$\left[\, pp_{-}p_{-}mp_{-}mf\,\right] f_{-}ff$

139

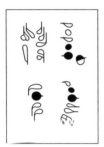

Notation

Pitch Content

Dynamic Range

$pp\left[\, p_{-}mp_{-}mf_{-}f_{-}ff\,\right]$

140

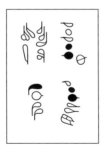

Notation

Pitch Content

Dynamic Range

$pp\left[\, p_{-}mp_{-}mf_{-}f\,\right] ff$

73

141

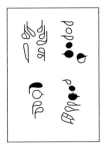

Notation

Pitch Content

Dynamic Range

$$\left[\,pp\!-\!p\!-\!mp\!-\!mf\!-\!f\!-\!ff\,\right]$$

142

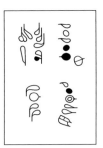

Notation

Pitch Content

Dynamic Range

$$pp\left[\,p\!-\!mp\!-\!mf\,\right]f\!-\!ff$$

143

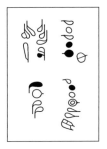

Notation

Pitch Content

Dynamic Range

$$\left[\,pp\!-\!p\!-\!mp\!-\!mf\!-\!f\!-\!ff\,\right]$$

144

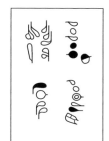

Pitch Content

Dynamic Range

$$\left[\, pp - p - mp - mf - f \,\right] f\!f$$

145

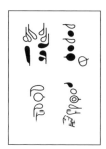

Notation

Pitch Content

Embouchure Suggestions
• High-Range Embouchure

Additional Notes
• Whisper Key Lock Required

Dynamic Range

$$pp \left[\, p - mp - mf - f \,\right] f\!f$$

5.2. Group Two: Monovalent Multiphonics

Group Two multiphonics often require more embouchure manipulations than Group One. They are still quite reliable. The dynamic range for Group Two multiphonics is slightly narrower in most cases, relative to Group One.

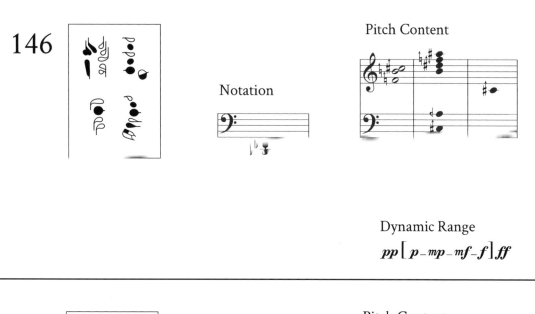

146

Notation

Pitch Content

Dynamic Range

$pp\left[\,p-mp-mf-f\,\right]ff$

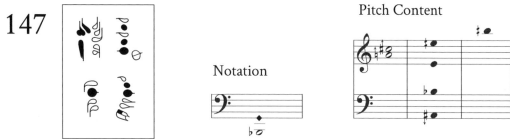

147

Notation

Pitch Content

Dynamic Range

$pp\left[\,p-mp-mf\,\right]f-ff$

148

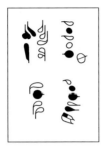

Pitch Content

Notation

Dynamic Range

pp [*p* – *mp* – *mf* – *f*] *ff*

149

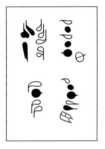

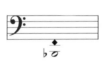

Pitch Content

Notation

Embouchure Suggestions:
• Firm Embouchure, Back of the Reed

Dynamic Range

pp – *p* [*mp* – *mf* – *f*] *ff*

150

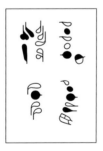

Pitch Content

Notation

Dynamic Range

pp [*p* – *mp* – *mf* – *f* – *ff*]

151

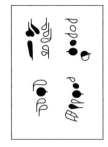

Pitch Content

Notation

Embouchure Suggestions
- Loose Embouchure
- Bocal Flex Down
- Open Throat

Dynamic Range

$pp\left[\,p-mp-mf-f\,\right]ff$

152

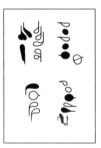

Pitch Content

Notation

Embouchure Suggestions
- Tight Pressure, Back of the Reed

Additional Notes
- Did not work on Püchner bassoons

Dynamic Range

$pp-p\left[\,mp\,\right]mf-f-ff$

153

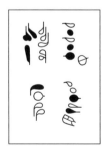

Pitch Content

Notation

Embouchure Suggestions
- Firm Embouchure, Back of the Reed
- Firm Embouchure, Middle of the Reed

Dynamic Range

$pp-p\left[\,mp-mf-f\,\right]ff$

154

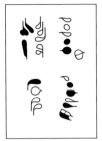

Notation

Pitch Content

Dynamic Range

pp–p–$mp\left[mf$–f–$ff\right]$

155

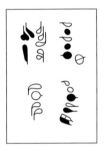

Notation

Pitch Content

Dynamic Range

$pp\left[p$–mp–mf–$f\right]ff$

156

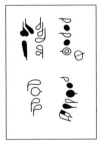

Notation

Pitch Content

Dynamic Range

$pp\left[p$–mp–mf–$f\right]ff$

80

157

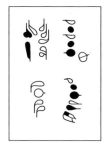

Pitch Content

Notation

Dynamic Range

$pp\left[\,p-mp-mf-f\,\right]ff$

158

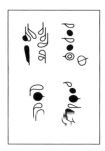

Pitch Content

Notation

Embouchure Suggestions
• Light Pressure, At the Collar

Dynamic Range

$\left[\,pp-p-mp-mf-f\,\right]ff$

159

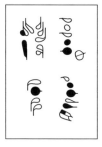

Pitch Content

Notation

Dynamic Range

$pp\left[\,p-mp-mf-f\,\right]ff$

160

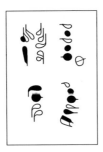

Pitch Content

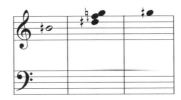

Notation

Dynamic Range

$pp\left[\,p-mp-mf-f\,\right]ff$

161

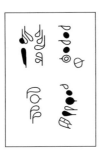

Pitch Content

Notation

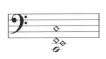

Dynamic Range

$pp\left[\,p-mp-mf-f\,\right]ff$

162

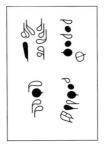

Pitch Content

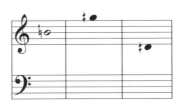

Notation

Embouchure Suggestions
- Vertical Pressure, Middle of the Reed
- Vertical Pressure, Back of the Reed

Dynamic Range

$pp\left[\,p-mp-mf\,\right]f-ff$

163

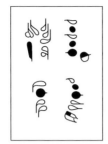

Pitch Content

Notation

Embouchure Suggestions
• Firm Pressure, Back of the Reed

Dynamic Range

$pp\,[\,p-mp-mf-f\,]\,ff$

164

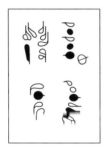

Pitch Content

Notation

Embouchure Suggestions
• Bocal Flex Down

Dynamic Range

$pp\,[\,p-mp-mf-f\,]\,ff$

165

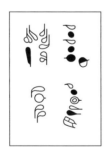

Pitch Content

Dynamic Range

$pp-p\,[\,mp-mf-f\,]\,ff$

166

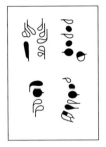

Pitch Content

Notation

Embouchure Suggestions
• Bocal Flex Down

Dynamic Range

$pp - p \left[mp - mf \right] f - f\!f$

167

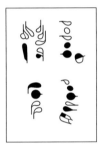

Pitch Content

Notation

Dynamic Range

$pp \left[p - mp - mf \right] f - f\!f$

168

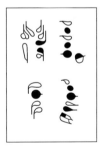

Pitch Content

Notation

Dynamic Range

$\left[pp - p - mp - mf \right] f - f\!f$

169

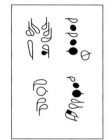

Notation

Pitch Content

Dynamic Range

$pp\left[\,p-mp-mf-f\,\right]ff$

170

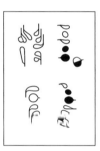

Notation

Pitch Content

Dynamic Range

$pp\left[\,p-mp-mf-f\,\right]ff$

171

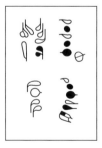

Notation

Pitch Content

Embouchure Suggestions
• Lowered Jaw, Open Throat

Dynamic Range

$pp\left[\,p-mp-mf-f\,\right]ff$

172

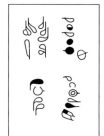

Pitch Content

Dynamic Range

$pp\,[\,p-mp-mf\,]\,f-ff$

173

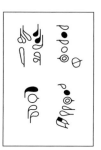

Pitch Content

Dynamic Range

$pp\,[\,p-mp-mf\,]\,f-ff$

174

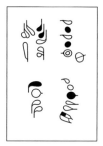

Pitch Content

Dynamic Range

$pp\,[\,p-mp-mf\,]\,f-ff$

175

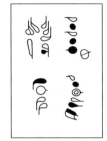

Notation

Pitch Content

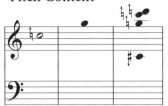

Embouchure Suggestions
- Firm Embouchure, At the Collar

Dynamic Range

$pp\left[\,p-mp-mf-f\,\right]ff$

176

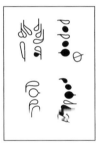

Notation

Pitch Content

For Composers
- Allow extra time to set this fingering
- May not be possible for bassoonists with small hands

Dynamic Range

$pp\left[\,p-mp-mf-f\,\right]ff$

177

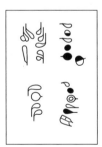

Pitch Content

Dynamic Range

$pp\left[\,p-mp-mf-f\,\right]ff$

178

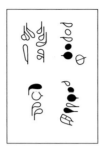

Pitch Content

Notation

Dynamic Range

$pp\,[\,p-mp-mf-f\,]\,ff$

179

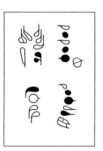

Pitch Content

Notation

Dynamic Range

$pp\,[\,p-mp-mf-f\,]\,ff$

180

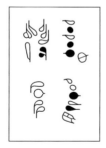

Pitch Content

Notation

Embouchure Suggestions
- Even Pressure, Both Blades

Dynamic Range

$pp\,[\,p-mp-mf-f\,]\,ff$

181

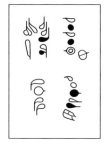

Notation

Pitch Content

Additional Notes
• Whisper Key Lock Required

Dynamic Range

$pp\,[\,p-mp-mf-f\,]\,ff$

182

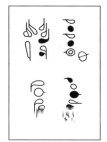

Notation

Pitch Content

Additional Notes
• Whisper Key Lock Required

Dynamic Range

$pp\,[\,p-mp-mf\,]\,f-ff$

183

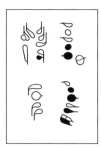

Notation

Pitch Content

Dynamic Range

$pp-p\,[\,mp-mf-f\,]\,ff$

184

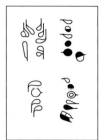

Pitch Content

Dynamic Range

$pp\left[\,p-mp-mf-f-ff\,\right]$

185

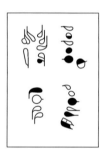

Pitch Content

Embouchure Suggestions
• Firm Embouchure, Middle of the Reed

Dynamic Range

$\left[\,pp-p-mp-mf-f\,\right]ff$

186

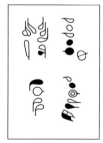

Notation

Pitch Content

Dynamic Range

$pp\left[\,p-mp-mf-f\,\right]ff$

187

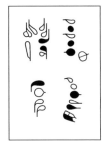

Notation

Pitch Content

Dynamic Range

$pp\left[\,p-mp-mf-f\,\right]ff$

188

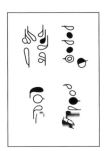

Embouchure Suggestions
• Firm Embouchure

Pitch Content

Dynamic Range

$pp\left[\,p-mp-mf-f\,\right]ff$

189

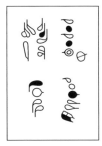

Pitch Content

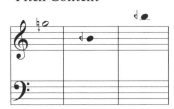

Dynamic Range

$pp\left[\,p-mp-mf\,\right]f-ff$

190

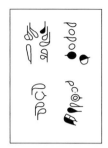

Pitch Content

Embouchure Suggestions
• High-Range Embouchure

Dynamic Range

$pp \left[p - mp - mf - f \right] ff$

191

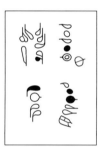

Notation

Pitch Content

Dynamic Range

$pp \left[p - mp - mf - f \right] ff$

192

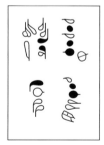

Notation

Pitch Content

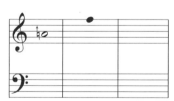

Embouchure Suggestions
• Pressure on Bottom Blade, as Little Pressure as Possible on Top Blade

Dynamic Range

$\left[pp - p - mp - mf - f \right] ff$

193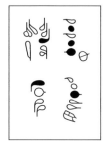

Notation

Pitch Content

Dynamic Range

pp [*p – mp – mf – f*] *ff*

194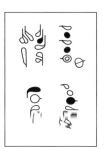

Notation

Pitch Content

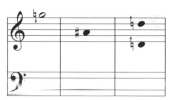

Dynamic Range

pp [*p – mp – mf*] *f – ff*

195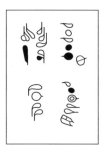

Notation

Pitch Content

Dynamic Range

pp [*p – mp – mf – f*] *ff*

196

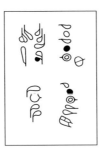

Notation

Pitch Content

Dynamic Range

$pp\left[\,p-mp-mf-f\,\right]\!f\!f$

197

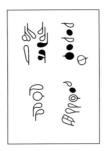

Notation

Pitch Content

Embouchure Suggestions
- High-Range Embouchure

Additional Notes
- Whisper Key Lock Required

Dynamic Range

$pp\left[\,p-mp-mf-f\,\right]\!f\!f$

198

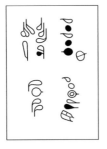

Notation

Pitch Content

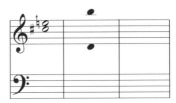

Embouchure Suggestions
- Head Tilted
- Firm Pressure, Middle of the Reed
- Firm Pressure, Back of the Reed

Dynamic Range

$pp-p\left[\,mp-mf-f\,\right]\!f\!f$

199

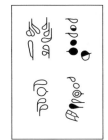

Pitch Content

Dynamic Range

$pp\left[\,p-mp-mf-f\,\right]ff$

200

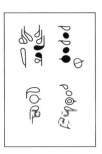

Notation

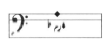

Pitch Content

Dynamic Range

$pp\left[\,p-mp-mf-f\,\right]ff$

201

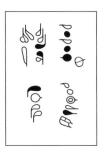

Notation

Pitch Content

Embouchure Suggestions
• Firm Pressure

Dynamic Range

$pp\left[\,p-mp-mf\,\right]f-ff$

202

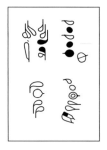

Notation

Pitch Content

Embouchure Suggestions
- Vertical Pressure, Back of the Reed

Dynamic Range

$[\,pp-p-mp-mf\,]f\!-\!f\!f$

203

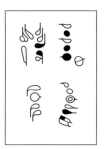

Notation

Pitch Content

Embouchure Suggestions
- Pressure on Bottom Blade

Dynamic Range

$[\,pp-p-mp\,]mf\!-\!f\!-\!f\!f$

204

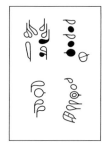

Notation

Pitch Content

Embouchure Suggestions
- High Tongue Placement
- Firm Embouchure

Additional Notes
- Whisper Key Lock Required

Dynamic Range

$[\,pp-p-mp-mf\!-\!f\,]f\!f$

5.3. Group Three: Monovalent Multiphonics

While they responded on a majority of instrument tested, Group Three multiphonics require the most embouchure manipulations of all the monovalent fingerings. Much like the extreme ranges of the instrument, these fingerings must be approached with caution, as they require specific embouchure settings. This group has the most restricted dynamic range; for several fingerings only one dynamic level is reliably produced.

205

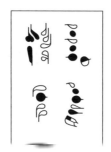

Notation

Pitch Content

Additional Notes
- Fox Bassoons – Firm Embouchure, Back of the Reed
- Püchner Bassoons – Did not produce a multiphonic

Dynamic Range

$pp\left[\,p-mp-mf\,\right]f\text{-}ff$

206

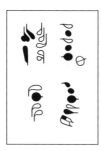

Notation

Pitch Content

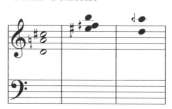

Embouchure Suggestions
- High-Range Embouchure

Additional Notes
- Bassoonists with small hands may not be able to reach this fingering

Dynamic Range

$\left[\,pp-p-mp-mf\,\right]f\text{-}ff$

207

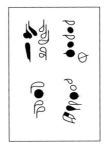

Pitch Content

Notation

Embouchure Suggestions
• Fox Bassoons – High-Range Embouchure

Dynamic Range

$pp\,[\,p-mp-mf-f\,]\,ff$

208

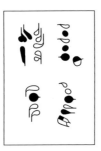

Pitch Content

Notation

Dynamic Range

$pp\,[\,p-mp-mf-f\,]\,ff$

209

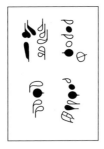

Pitch Content

Notation

Embouchure Suggestions
• Vertical Pressure, Middle of the Reed

Dynamic Range

$pp-p\,[\,mp-mf-f\,]\,ff$

210

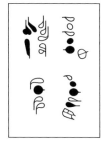

Pitch Content

Notation

Embouchure Suggestions
• Lowered Jaw

Dynamic Range

$pp\left[\,p\!-\!mp\!-\!mf\,\right]f\!-\!f\!f$

211

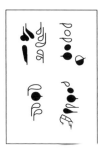

Pitch Content

Notation

Dynamic Range

$pp\left[\,p\!-\!mp\!-\!mf\,\right]f\!-\!f\!f$

212

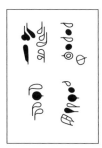

Pitch Content

Notation

Dynamic Range

$pp\left[\,p\!-\!mp\!-\!mf\!-\!f\,\right]f\!f$

213

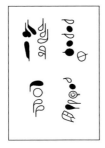

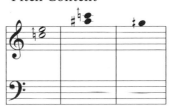

Pitch Content

Notation

Embouchure Suggestions
• Firm Pressure, At the Collar

Dynamic Range

pp–p [mp–mf] f–ff

214

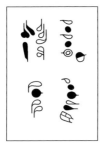

Pitch Content

Notation

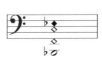

Additional Notes
• Produces distinctly different pitch content over the dynamic spectrum

Dynamic Range

[pp–p–mp–mf–f–ff]

215

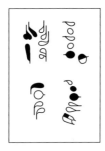

Pitch Content

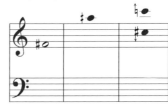

Embouchure Suggestions
• High-Range Embouchure

Dynamic Range

[pp–p–mp–mf–f–ff]

100

216

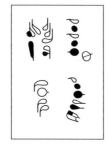

Notation

Pitch Content

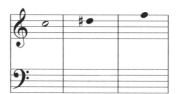

Additional Notes
• Whisper Key Lock Required

Dynamic Range

$pp\left[\,p-mp-mf\,\right]f-ff$

217

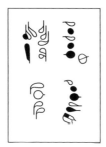

Notation

Pitch Content

Embouchure Suggestions
• Firm, Even Pressure, At the Collar

Dynamic Range

$pp\left[\,p-mp-mf\,\right]f-ff$

218

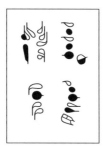

Notation

Pitch Content

Embouchure Suggestions
• Firm Pressure, Bottom Blade
• Firm Pressure, Both Blades

Dynamic Range

$pp-p\left[\,mp-mf-f\,\right]ff$

219

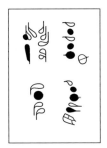

Pitch Content

Notation

Dynamic Range

$pp\text{–}p\left[\,mp\text{–}mf\,\right]f\text{–}ff$

220

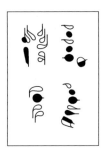

Pitch Content

Notation

Dynamic Range

$pp\left[\,p\text{–}mp\text{–}mf\text{–}f\,\right]ff$

221

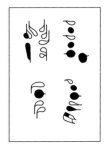

Pitch Content

Notation

Additional Notes
• Fox Bassoons – Did not produce a multiphonic

Dynamic Range

$pp\text{–}p\left[\,mp\,\right]mf\text{–}f\text{–}ff$

222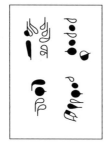

Notation

Pitch Content

Embouchure Suggestions
• Firm, Even Pressure, At the Collar

Dynamic Range

pp – p – mp [*mf*] *f – ff*

223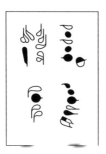

Notation

Pitch Content

Dynamic Range

pp [*p – mp – mf – f*] *ff*

224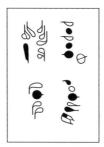

Notation

Pitch Content

Dynamic Range

pp [*p – mp – mf*] *f – ff*

225

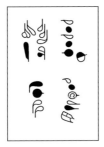

Pitch Content

Notation

Embouchure Suggestions
 • High-Range Embouchure

Dynamic Range

$pp-p\left[mp-mf-f\right]ff$

226

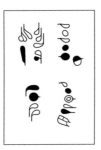

Pitch Content

Notation

Dynamic Range

$pp\left[p-mp-mf-f\right]ff$

227

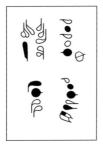

Pitch Content

Notation

Embouchure Suggestions
 • Tight Embouchure, At the Collar

Dynamic Range

$pp\left[p-mp-mf-f\right]ff$

228

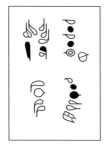

Pitch Content

Notation

Embouchure Suggestions
• Bocal Flex Up

Dynamic Range

$pp \left[p - mp - mf \right] f - ff$

229

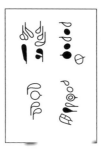

Pitch Content

Notation

Embouchure Suggestions
• Firm Embouchure, Back of the Reed

Dynamic Range

$pp \left[p - mp - mf \right] f - ff$

230

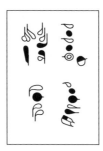

Pitch Content

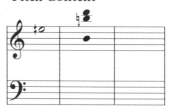

Notation

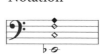

Embouchure Suggestions
• High-Range Embouchure

Dynamic Range

$pp - p - mp \left[mf \right] f - ff$

231

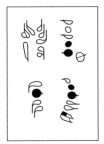

Notation

Pitch Content

Dynamic Range

$pp\left[\,p-mp-mf-f\,\right]ff$

232

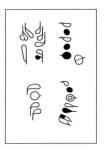

Notation

Pitch Content

Embouchure Suggestions
• Slight Pressure, Both Blades

Dynamic Range

$pp\left[\,p-mp-mf\,\right]f-ff$

233

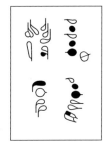

Notation

Pitch Content

Embouchure Suggestions
• Firm Embouchure
• Head Tilted

Additional Notes
• Püchner Bassoons - Did not produce a multiphonic

Dynamic Range

$pp-p\left[\,mp-mf-f\,\right]ff$

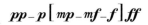

234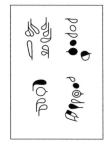

Notation

Pitch Content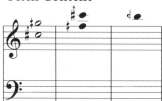

Embouchure Suggestions
  • Firm Pressure, Back of the Reed

Dynamic Range

$$\left[\, pp - p - mp - mf - f - ff \,\right]$$

235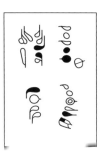

Pitch Content

Dynamic Range

$$pp \left[\, p - mp \,\right] mf - f - ff$$

236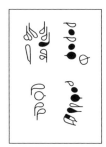

Notation

Pitch Content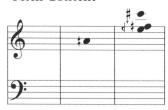

Embouchure Suggestions
  • Firm Pressure, Both Blades

Dynamic Range

$$pp \left[\, p - mp - mf - f \,\right] ff$$

237

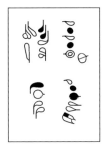

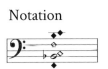

Notation

Pitch Content

Dynamic Range

pp [*p* – *mp*] *mf* – *f* – *ff*

238

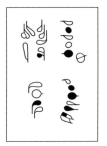

Notation

Pitch Content

Embouchure Suggestions
• Lowered Jaw

Dynamic Range

pp [*p* – *mp*] *mf* – *f* – *ff*

239

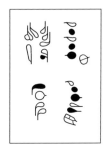

Notation

Pitch Content

Embouchure Suggestions
• High-Range Embouchure

Dynamic Range

pp [*p* – *mp* – *mf*] *f* – *ff*

240

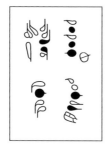

Notation

Pitch Content

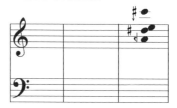

Dynamic Range

$pp \left[p-mp-mf \right] f\!-\!f\!f$

241

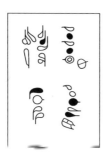

Notation

Pitch Content

Embouchure Suggestions
• Firm Pressure, At the Collar

Dynamic Range

$pp-p \left[mp-mf \right] f\!-\!f\!f$

242

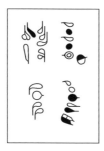

Notation

Pitch Content

Dynamic Range

$pp \left[p-mp-mf\!-\!f\!-\!f\!f \right]$

243

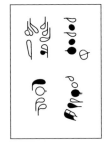

Notation

Pitch Content

Embouchure Suggestions
• Pressure on Bottom Blade
• Head Tilted

Dynamic Range

pp – p – mp [mf – f] ff

244

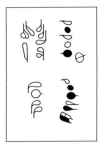

Notation

Pitch Content

Dynamic Range

pp – p [mp – mf] f – ff

245

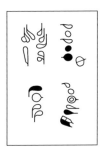

Pitch Content

Dynamic Range

pp – p [mp – mf – f] ff

246

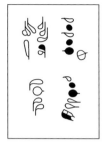

Notation

Pitch Content

Dynamic Range

pp–*p*–*mp* [*mf*–*f*] *ff*

247

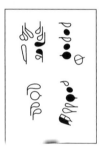

Notation

Pitch Content

Embouchure Suggestions
- High-Range Embouchure
- Vertical Pressure

Dynamic Range

pp [*p*–*mp*–*mf*] *f*–*ff*

248

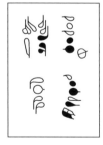

Notation

Pitch Content

Additional Notes
- Whisper Key Lock Required

Dynamic Range

pp–*p* [*mp*–*mf*–*f*] *ff*

249

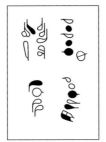

Pitch Content

Dynamic Range

$pp - p \left[mp - mf - f - ff \right]$

250

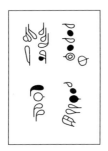

Notation

Pitch Content

Additional Notes
• Püchner Bassoons – Did not produce a multiphonic

Dynamic Range

$pp \left[p - mp - mf \right] f - ff$

251

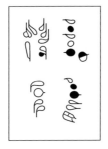

Notation

Pitch Content

Embouchure Suggestions
• High-Range Embouchure

Dynamic Range

$\left[pp - p - mp - mf - f - ff \right]$

112

252

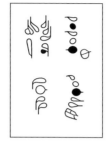

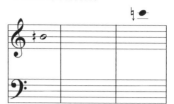

Pitch Content

Notation

Embouchure Suggestions
• High-Range Embouchure

Dynamic Range

$pp\left[\,p\text{--}mp\text{--}mf\,\right]f\text{--}ff$

253

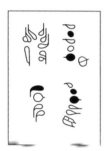

Pitch Content

Notation

Embouchure Suggestions
• Firm Pressure, At the Collar

Dynamic Range

$pp\left[\,p\text{--}mp\,\right]mf\text{--}f\text{--}ff$

254

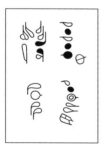

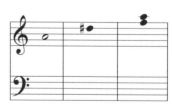

Pitch Content

Notation

Dynamic Range

$pp\left[\,p\text{--}mp\text{--}mf\text{--}f\,\right]ff$

255

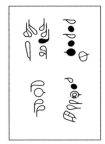

Notation

Pitch Content

Dynamic Range

pp–*p* [*mp*] *mf*–*f*–*ff*

256

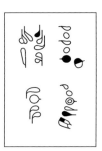

Embouchure Suggestions
• High-Range Embouchure

Pitch Content

Dynamic Range

pp [*p*–*mp*–*mf*–*f*] *ff*

5.4. Group Four: Polyvalent Multiphonics

Group Four multiphonics are produced by manipulating standard fingerings (see Section 2.3). These fingerings work on all instruments, and can be accomplished by performers with at least one year of experience. These fingerings all have a full dynamic range.

Low-Range Polyvalent Fingerings

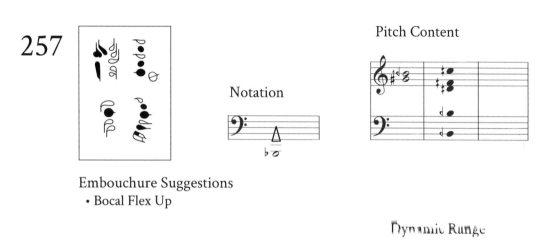

257

Notation

Pitch Content

Embouchure Suggestions
• Bocal Flex Up

Dynamic Range

$[\,pp-p-mp-mf-f-ff\,]$

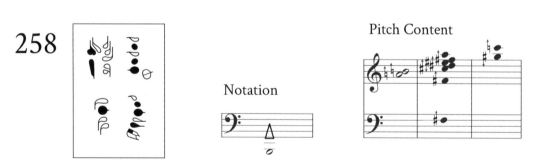

258

Notation

Pitch Content

Embouchure Suggestions
• Bocal Flex Up

Dynamic Range

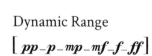

$[\,pp-p-mp-mf-f-ff\,]$

259

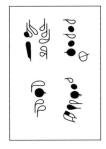

Pitch Content

Notation

Embouchure Suggestions
• Bocal Flex Up

Dynamic Range

$\left[\,pp - p - mp - mf - f - ff\,\right]$

260

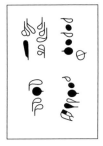

Pitch Content

Notation

Embouchure Suggestions
• Bocal Flex Up

Dynamic Range

$\left[\,pp - p - mp - mf - f - ff\,\right]$

261

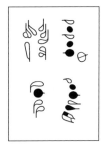

Pitch Content

Notation

Embouchure Suggestions
• Bocal Flex Up

Dynamic Range

$\left[\,pp - p - mp - mf - f - ff\,\right]$

High-Range Polyvalent Fingerings

262

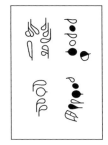

Notation

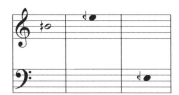

Pitch Content

Embouchure Suggestions
• Bocal Flex Down

Dynamic Range

$\left[\, pp - p - mp - mf - f - ff \,\right]$

263

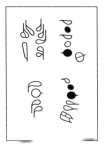

Notation

Pitch Content

Embouchure Suggestions
• Bocal Flex Down

Dynamic Range

$\left[\, pp - p - mp - mf - f - ff \,\right]$

264

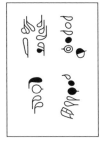

Notation

Pitch Content

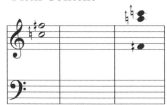

Embouchure Suggestions
• Bocal Flex Down

Dynamic Range

$\left[\, pp - p - mp - mf - f - ff \,\right]$

265

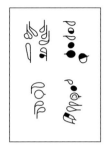

Notation

Pitch Content

Embouchure Suggestions
• Bocal Flex Down

Dynamic Range

$\left[\,pp-p-mp-mf-f-ff\,\right]$

266

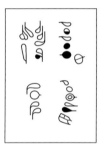

Notation

Pitch Content

Embouchure Suggestions
• Bocal Flex Down

Dynamic Range

$\left[\,pp-p-mp-mf-f-ff\,\right]$

267

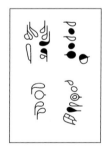

Notation

Pitch Content

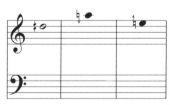

Embouchure Suggestions
• Bocal Flex Down

Dynamic Range

$\left[\,pp-p-mp-mf-f-ff\,\right]$

268

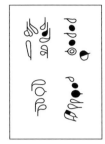

Embouchure Suggestions
• Bocal Flex Down

Notation

Pitch Content

Dynamic Range

$[\ pp - p - mp - mf - f - ff\ ]$

269

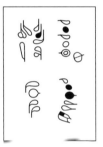

Embouchure Suggestions
• Bocal Flex Down

Notation

Pitch Content

Dynamic Range

$[\ pp - p - mp - mf - f - ff\ ]$

270

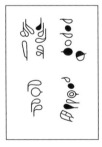

Embouchure Suggestions
• Bocal Flex Down

Notation

Pitch Content

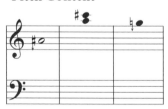

Dynamic Range

$[\ pp - p - mp - mf - f - ff\ ]$

271

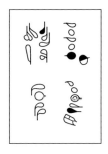

Embouchure Suggestions
• Bocal Flex Down

Notation

Pitch Content

Dynamic Range

$\left[\, \boldsymbol{pp} - \boldsymbol{p} - \boldsymbol{mp} - \boldsymbol{mf} - \boldsymbol{f} - \boldsymbol{ff} \,\right]$

Bibliography

Books

Bartolozzi, Bruno. *New Sounds for Woodwind*. Reginald Smith Brindle, translator. New York: Oxford University Press, 1967.

Bombardier, Bradley A. *Notation for Contemporary Double-Reed Techniuqes a Guide for Composers and Performers*. Masters Thesis, Bowling Green State University, 1984.

Dick, Robert. *The Other Flute*. Multiple Breaths Music Company, 1989.

Gallois, Pascal. *The Techniques of Bassoon Playing*. New York: Bärenreiter, 2009.

Kelley, Cheryl K. *Twentieth century bassoon techniques*. Masters Thesis, University of Nebraska, 1987.

Lipp, Charles Herbert. *New Compositional Techniques for the Bassoon*. Masters Thesis, University of Illinois at Urbana-Champaign, 1982.

Netti, Giorgio and Marcus Weiss. *The Techniques of Saxophone Playing*. New York: Bärenreiter, 2010.

Ouzounoff, Alexandre. *Actuellement le Basson*. Paris: Editions Slabert, 1986.

Penazzi, Sergio. *Metodo Per Fagotto*. Milan: Suvini Zerboni, 1972.

Read, Gardner. *Compendium of Contemporary Instrumental Techniques*. New York: Schirmer Books, 1976.

Rehfeldt, Phillip. *New Directions for Clarinet*. Lanham, Maryland: Scarecrow Press, 1994.

Van Cleve, Libby. *Oboe Unbound*. Lanham, Maryland: Scarecrow Press, 2004.

Vonk, Maarten. *A Bundle of Joy: A Practical Handbook for the Bassoon*. Amersfoort, Netherland: Fagot Atelier Maarten Vonk, 2007.

Waterhouse, William. *The Bassoon*. London: Kahn & Avrill, 2003.

Articles

Backus, John. "Multiphonic tones in the woodwind instruments." *Journal of the Acoustical Society of America* 63, no. 2 (1978): 591–599.

Barata, Antonio G. "Sources of Information on Woodwind Multiphonics: An Annotated Bibliography." *Perspectives of New Music* 26, no. 1 (1988): 246–256.

Burns, Michael. "Response Issues on the Bassoon: Cracking Low Notes, Cracking High Notes, Bocal Flex – Voicing – Foghorn Effect." *The Double Reed* 30, no. 4 (2007): 71–75.

Heiss, John C. "Multiple-Sonorities for Flute, Oboe, Clarinet, and Bassoon." *Perspectives of New Music*, Vol. 7, No. 1 (1968): 136–142.

Sampson, Jamie Leigh. "Polyvalent Fingerings for the Bassoon: An Introduction." *The Double Reed*, Vol. 37, No. 1 (2014): 134–142.

Websites

University of Michigan Bassoon Studio, s.v. "New Music for and with Bassoon" (by Jeffrey Lyman) http://www-personal.umich.edu/~jlym/pages/new_bsn_intro.html (accessed November 29, 2013).

International Double Reed Society website, s.v. "Heckel-System (German) Bassoon Multiphonic Fingerings by Note Name" (by Terry Ewell), http://www.idrs.org/resources/BSNFING/fingmult.htm (accessed November 29, 2013).

Leslie Ross's official Web site, s.v. "Multiphonics for Modern Bassoon" (by Leslie Ross), http://www.leslieross.net/multiphonics.html (accessed November 29, 2013).

Appendix A: Multiphonic Reference Table

Number	IDRS	Penazzi	Gallois	Lipp	Ross	Bartolozzi	Christlieb
1				•	•		•
2		•					
3					•		
4					•		
5					•		
6					•		
7			•				
8					•		
9			•		•	•	
10			•		•		
11					•		
12			•		•		
13			•				
14			•		•		
15			•				
16	•			•			•
17			•				
18	•						
19					•		
20				•	•		
21	•						
22	•						
23					•		
24					•		
25					•		
26					•		
27				•			
28				•			
29	•						
30					•		
31			•				
32				•	•		
33	•	•				•	
34				•			
35					•		
36				•	•		
37					•		
38				•			•
39				•			

Number	IDRS	Penazzi	Gallois	Lipp	Ross	Bartolozzi	Christlieb
40				•		•	
41				•			
42			•				
43						•	
44						•	
45						•	
46						•	
47						•	
48						•	
49		•			•		
50						•	
51						•	
52						•	
53		•					
54					•		
55						•	
56						•	
57			•				
58			•				
59			•			•	
60				•	•	•	
61					•		
62					•		
63	•						
64	•						•
65	•					•	
66	•				•		
67						•	
68	•						•
69			•			•	
70	•	•			•	•	•
71	•						•
72						•	
73		•				•	•
74						•	•
75	•						
76	•					•	
77	•				•	•	•
78					•		
79	•				•	•	•
80					•	•	
81					•	•	
82		•				•	

Number	IDRS	Penazzi	Gallois	Lipp	Ross	Bartolozzi	Christlieb
83						•	
84	•						
85						•	
86					•	•	
87						•	
88						•	
89	•	•	•		•	•	
90						•	
91	•				•		
92					•		
93		•	•				
94		•				•	
95						•	
96						•	
97		•					
98		•				•	
99					•		
100			•			•	
101						•	
102						•	
103		•			•	•	
104						•	
105		•					
106		•					
107		•	•		•	•	
108						•	
109	•						•
110					•	•	•
111	•	•			•		•
112						•	
113						•	
114	•						
115							
116	•						
117		•				•	
118							
119					•		
120	•						•
121	•						
122		•				•	
123						•	
124	•	•				•	
125							

Number	IDRS	Penazzi	Gallois	Lipp	Ross	Bartolozzi	Christlieb
126			•				•
127						•	
128						•	
129		•				•	•
130						•	
131	•		•	•			
132	•					•	
133	•	•		•			•
134				•			
135						•	
136		•				•	
137		•					
138		•				•	
139	•						•
140	•					•	•
141	•		•	•			•
142			•	•			
143			•			•	
144	•						
145				•			
Group 2							
146				•			
147	•			•		•	
148				•			
149	•			•			
150	•						
151	•						
152		•					
153		•					
154	•						
155						•	
156						•	
157						•	•
158				•			
159						•	
160						•	
161	•						
162				•			
163				•			
164	•			•		•	•
165						•	
166						•	
167						•	

Number	IDRS	Penazzi	Gallois	Lipp	Ross	Bartolozzi	Christlieb
168				•			
169						•	
170						•	
171			•	•		•	
172						•	
173						•	
174						•	
175						•	
176				•			
177	•						•
178	•					•	
179						•	
180						•	
181						•	
182						•	
183					•	•	
184	•						•
185							
186						•	
187						•	
188			•			•	
189						•	
190			•				
191						•	
192					•	•	
193						•	
194						•	
195						•	
196						•	
197						•	
198			•			•	
199						•	
200						•	
201						•	
202			•				
203			•				
204					•		•
Group 3							
205					•		
206					•		
207					•		
208						•	
209	•						

Number	IDRS	Penazzi	Gallois	Lipp	Ross	Bartolozzi	Christlieb
210	•						
211	•						
212	•						
213		•					
214	•						
215							
216					•		
217				•			
218				•			
219				•			
220					•		
221				•			
222				•	•		
223				•			
224					•		
225					•		
226					•		
227							
228					•		
229				•			
230				•			
231					•		
232				•	•		
233	•			•	•		
234	•						
235			•				
236	•					•	•
237					•		
238				•			
239					•		
240			•				
241					•		
242			•				
243					•		
244					•		
245					•		
246					•		
247					•		
248					•		
249			•				
250	•			•			•
251	•	•	•	•	•	•	
252					•		

Number	IDRS	Penazzi	Gallois	Lipp	Ross	Bartolozzi	Christlieb
253		•			•		•
254				•			
255		•		•			
256							
Group 4							
257			•	•			
258			•	•			
259			•	•			
260							
261							
262			•	•			•
263			•	•			•
264			•				•
265			•				•
266			•				•
267			•				•
268			•				•
269							
270			•				
271							

Appendix B: Multiphonics Categorized by Prominent Pitch

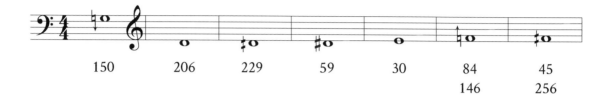

150	206	229	59	30	84	45
					146	256

215	53	40	232	44	104	181	17
	164	43				257	40
		93					106
							136
							186
							207

1	2	20	21	270	41	111	1
119	16	69	134		42		18
120	110	145	156		65		70
168	197	147			81		71
182	200	192			135		131
206	204	258			138		132
	248						137
	254						188
							205
							257

32	4	112	26	14	28	36
159	57	115	34	21	35	37
238	82	140	91	51	42	54
	130	146	133	142	89	66
	208	149	141	161	140	92
	233	162	160	195	216	164
		171	167	222	253	165
		237	209	239		173
		250	210			175
		251	212			191
		258	218			196
		263	219			213
			231			217
			252			227
			261			260
			262			264

13	17	7	12	2	25	5
31	33	27	69	8	29	9
86	58	38	73	10	68	20
100	64	93	78	15	144	39
143	77	107	88	32	169	70
155	87	113	101	40	224	105
	94	126	146	128	256	106
	103	198	147	172	271	117
	119	206	158	176		
	183	207	234			
		249	242			
			266			

System 1

60	1	16	6	14	39	30
61	65	168	11	21	54	40
62	91	178	22	66	81	72
80	267	211	36	67	153	79
82			157	177	220	98
85			158	214		102
111			205			133
261			265			213
						251

System 2

77	19	12	114	29	87	166
118	23	24	121	63	116	
129	96	27	139	84	125	
149	122	115	201	161	129	
184	127		217		141	
198	150				264	
232	230					

System 3

49	48	4	32	55	65	12
68	75	41	54	64	111	47
70		42	59	79	194	56
71		43	108	93		129
170		76	183	178		148
223		109	189			153
		137	194			154
		164				234
		185				268

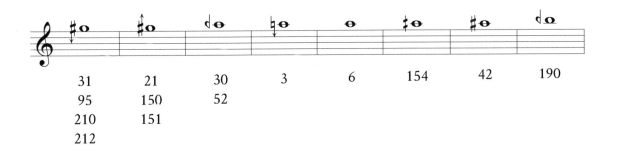

31	21	30	3	6	154	42	190
95	150	52					
210	151						
212							

17	76	105	84	81	54	235	190
249	107	174		114	269		
	233						

Appendix C: Selected Compositions with Multiphonics

Solo Bassoon • Bassoon & Piano • Bassoon & Electronics

Aho, Kalevi. *Solo V*. Helinski, Finland: Fennica Gehrman, 1999.

Balter, Marcos. *...And Also a Fountain*. Self-published, 2012.

Berio, Luciano. *Sequenza XII*. New York: Universal Edition, 1998.

Boulez, Pierre. *Dialogue de l'obre double*. New York: Universal Edition, 1984.

Burns, Michael. *Swamp Song*. Self-published, 1986.

Davis, Nathan. *On Speaking 100 Names*. Self-published, 2010.

De Oca, Ramon Montes. *Laberinto de Espejos*. Peermusic, 1990.

del Aguila, Miguel. *Sunset Song*. Self-published, 1994.

Ewell, Terry B. *Gethsemane*. Self-published, 1985.

Fagerlund, Sebastian. *Woodlands*. London: Edition Peters, 2012.

Fujikura, Dai. *Calling*. Berlin: Ricordi Berlin, 2011.

Guzman, Edgar. ∞¿?. Self-published, 2008.

————— *Prologue*. Self-published, 2013.

Hersant, Philippe. *Niggun*. Paris: Durand Editions Musicales, 1995.

————— *Hopi*. Paris: Durand Editions Musicales, 1994.

Hovatter, Kyle. *Mist*. Medina, New York: Imagine Music Publishing, 2011.

————— *En Los Bosques*. Medina, New York: Imagine Music Publishing, 2012.

Kaplan, Amelia. *BLOW*. Tallevast, FL: Trevco, 2001.

Krauss, Morgan. *Divide Its White Laughter Into Two*. Self-published, 2014.

Mantovani, Bruno. *Un mois d'octobre*. Paris: Editions Henry Lemoine, 2001.

Omiccioli, Nicholas. *insights no. 1*. Self-published, 2009.

Ronneau, Jesse. *Portée*. Self-published, 2012.

Sampson, Jamie Leigh. *Frozen Landscape*. Bowling Green, OH: ADJ•ective New Music, LLC, 2008.

Schoeller, Philippe. *Isis II*. Paris: Édition musicales europénnes, 2006.

Smith, Andrew Martin. *Nexus*. Bowling Green, OH: ADJ•ective New Music, LLC, 2010.

Steinmetz, John. Three Etudes. Tallevast, FL: Trevco, 1975.

Toledo, Marcelo. *Qualia 2*. Self-published, 2012.

Ward-Steinman, David. *Childs Play*. New York: E.C. Schirmier, 1974.

Weait, Christopher. *Variations for Solo Bassoon*. Harmuse Publications, 1975.

Winstead, William. *Enigma*. Tallevast, FL: Trevco, 1976.

Wolfgang, Gernot. *Dual Identity*. Vienna: Doblinger Music Publishers, 2005.

Zavala, Ernesto. *Into Versión*. Self-published, 2009.

Chamber Ensembles

Dietz, Christopher. *Thicket*. Self-published, 2011.

Fujikura, Dai. *Phantom Splinter*. Berlin: Ricordi, 2009.

———— *The Voice*. London: Ricordi Berlin, 2007.

Gubaidulina, Sofia. *Duo Sonata*. Hamburg: H. Sikorski, 1998.

————*Hommage à T.S. Eliot*. Hamburg: H. Sikorski, 1991.

————*Quasi hoquetus*. Hamburg: H. Sikorski, 1985.

Hersant, Philippe. *8 Duos*. Paris: Durand Editions Musicales, 1995.

Kirsten, Amy Beth. *World Under Glass No. 1*. Self-Published, 2011.

Neuwirth, Olga. *In Nacht und Eis*. New York: Boosey & Hawkes, 2007.

————*Torsion: Transparent Variation*. New York: Boosey & Hawkes, 2001.

Sampson, Jamie Leigh. *Strife*. Bowling Green, OH: ADJ•ective New Music, 2013.

Schoeller, Philippe. *Lamento*. Paris: Édition musicales europénnes, 2002.

Concerti

Fujikura, Dai. *Bassoon Concerto*. Berlin: Ricordi Berlin, 2012.

Gubaidulina, Sofia. *Concerto for bassoon and low strings*. Hamburg: H. Sikorski, 1993.

Neuwirth, Olga. *Zefiro aleggia... nell'infinito*. New York: Boosey & Hawkes, 2004.

Made in the USA
Middletown, DE
29 December 2021

57253152R00088